Police and Naxalism
Strategies for Solutions

Police and Naxalism
Strategies for Solutions

ML Kumawat, IPS
Former: DG – BSF

Dr Nazrul Islam, IPS

Manas Publications
(We Convert Fighters into Writers)
New Delhi-110 002 (INDIA)

MANAS PUBLICATIONS
(Publishers, Library Suppliers, Importers & Exporters)
4402/5-A, Ansari Road (Opp. HDFC Bank)
Darya Ganj, New Delhi-110 002 (INDIA)
Off. ✆ 23260783, 23265523, Res. ✆ 23842660
Fax: 011-23272766
E-mail: manaspublications@vsnl.com
manaspublications@yahoo.com

ISBN 978-81-7049-318-1

Rs **595**

Typeset at

Manas Publications

Printed in India at
RK Print Services, Delhi
and published by Mrs Suman Lata for
Manas Publications, 4402/5-A, Ansari Road
(Opp. HDFC Bank),
Darya Ganj, New Delhi-110 002 (INDIA)

Contents

Preface

The advent of Indian Independence transformed the political governance system, but the police system retained its colonial underpinnings. The liabilities and duties of the police, in the present democratic system are more socialistic in comparison to the other types of governments. Police being an integral part of the government, its actions are concerned with the detection of crime, maintaining law and order besides enforcing social legislations and also to protect the weak and the defenceless. Those who seek to promote communal violence and discord have to be dealt with firmly.

However, the years after independence witnessed the enactment of new legislation in several states of the country. The first to come into force was the Bombay Police Act of 1951, which also governs the police forces in Maharashtra and Gujarat. Next was the Kerala Police Act of 1960, followed by the Karnataka Police Act of 1863 and then the Delhi Police Act of 1978. Recently the government of Madhya Pradesh framed a Police Bill 2002. These new Acts were based almost on the model of Police Act of 1861. But much more needs to be done to streamline the Police organisation. A critical approach to the problems and difficulties could prove extremely useful.

The present book is a collection of desperate articles which bring into fore various situations, multifaceted problems and difficulties that come in the way of better policing *vis a vis* constitutional liabilities concerning the criminal justice and demands meaningful academic interactions for making the police as people friendly. The contributors have given practical suggestions to improve the present Indian legal system and the police set-up as well.

At present, the country is facing three challenges to internal security, i.e. terrorism, insurgency in the North-East, and thirdly Leftwing extremism or Naxalism. On more than one occasion, the Prime Minister has rightly cautioned the nation that Naxalism posed the "single biggest internal security challenge" to India. Police is the instrument to confront and defeat these challenges.

The articles present a kaleidoscopic view of the police and the Indian reality, in the present global as well as country's internal scenario, and strive to grapple with some of the basic issues which create dilemmas for the police as a service organisation. All the writers with their vast experience and expertise in various fields have given an analytical view of modern policing trends. It is firmly hoped that the law enforcement officers will thoroughly go through these articles and will try their best to modernise the working of the Indian Police so that a healthy tradition of public cooperation may develop in future.

1

Police in India

Constitutional Position and the Criminal Justice System

Constitutional Position

INDIA is a union of 28 states and seven union territories. The powers and responsibilities of the union and states are demarcated in the Constitution of India. Article 246 of the Constitution distributes the legislative powers between the Parliament and the state legislative assemblies. It refers to three lists of subjects given in the Seventh Schedule of the Constitution:

List 1: Union List: includes subjects in respect of which the Parliament has the sole power to make laws.

List 2: State List: includes subjects in respect of which the state legislature has exclusive powers to make laws.

List 3: Concurrent List: consisting of subjects on which both the Parliament and the state legislatures have concurrent powers to make laws.

Article 246 of the Constitution of India places the police, public order, courts, prisons, reformatories, borstal and other allied institutions in the state list.

The police is a state subject and its organisation and working are governed by the rules and regulations framed by the state governments. These rules and regulations are outlined in the Police Manuals of the state police forces.

Each State/Union Territory has its separate police force.

Despite the diversity of police forces, there is a good deal that is common amongst them. This is due to four main reasons:

- The structure and working of the state police forces are governed by the Police Act of 1861, which is applicable in most parts of the country, or by the State Police Acts modelled mostly on the 1861 legislation.
- Major criminal laws, like the Indian Penal Code, the Code of Criminal Procedure, and the Indian Evidence Act are uniformly applicable to almost all parts of the country.
- The Indian Police Service (IPS) is an All India Service, which is recruited, trained and managed by the Central Government and which provides the bulk of senior officers to the state police forces.
- The quasi-federal character of the Indian polity, with specific provisions in the Constitution, allows a coordinating and counselling role for the centre in police matters and even authorizes it to set up certain central police organisations.

Police Legislation

Pre-Independence: The Police Act of 1861 remains the central piece of legislation that governs all aspects of policing in India. Much of police work is also administered by the Indian Penal Code (IPC), the Code of Criminal Procedure (Cr.PC) and the Indian Evidence Act 1872. The 1861 Act was established directly after the Indian Independence movement of 1857. The experience of such firm resistance led the colonial rulers to impose a regime police force upon their subjects, which could be used solely to consolidate and perpetuate their rule in the country. In fact, the 1861 Act instituted a police system designed to be absolutely subservient to the executive and highly authoritarian. The managerial philosophy of the police hierarchy was based on lack of confidence of the lower ranks.

Post-Independence: The advent of Indian independence transformed the political system, but the police system retained its colonial underpinnings. The Police Act of 1861 was not replaced. Political control over the police remained intact. The managerial philosophy, value system, and ethos of the police has remained militaristic in design.

The years after independence witnessed the enactment of new legislation in several states of the country. The first to come into force was the Bombay Police Act of 1951, which also governs the police forces in Maharashtra and Gujarat. Next was the Kerala Police Act of 1960, followed by the Karnataka Police Act of 1963, and lastly the Delhi Police Act of 1978. Most recently, the government of Madhya Pradesh framed a Police Bill 2002. These new Acts were patterned almost exactly on the model of the 1861 Act, resulting in no significant improvement in the performance of the police forces.

Criminal Justice System

Understanding the criminal justice system is a prelude to understanding the police. It is important to discuss a few important characteristics of the system before explaining the organisation and working of the police in India.

Criminal Law: The criminal law consists of the substantive law contained in the Indian Penal Code (IPC) as well as the special and local laws enacted by the central and state legislatures from time to time and the procedural law laid down mainly in the Code of Criminal Procedure, 1973 (CrPC) and the Indian Evidence Act 1872.

These three major Acts, i.e. the IPC, CrPC and the Indian Evidence Act were enacted by the British during the second half of the 19th century. Of these, the only major law that has been revised since Independence is the CrPC, which was revised in 1973 on the recommendations made by the Law Commission of India. The other two laws, except for some minor amendments, have remained unchanged.

Substantive Law: The IPC defines different types of crimes and prescribes appropriate punishment for offences. Offences are classified under different categories: offences against state, armed forces, public order, public justice, public health, safety, morals, human body, property and offences relating to elections, coins, government stamps, weights and measures, religion, documents and property marks, marriage and defamation. The IPC has 511 Sections, of which 330 are about punishments.

Besides IPC, the local and special laws (SLL)[1] also contain penal provisions. These laws have been enacted from time to time mainly to deal with new emerging forms of crime and to protect the interests of the weaker sections of society. A large number of criminal offences are registered under these laws, some of which relate to possession and manufacture of arms, ammunition and explosives; drugs; gambling; immoral trafficking in women; atrocities against scheduled castes and tribes; excise and prohibition; smuggling; hoarding and profiteering in essential commodities; food adulteration; traffic offences, etc.

Procedural Law: Procedural law describes the procedure to be followed in a criminal case from registration, investigation and to its final disposal after a proper trial by a court of law. The police are not empowered to take cognizance of all penal offences. Criminal law makes a distinction between two categories of offences, cognizable and non-cognizable[2].

The Process of Criminal Justice

The process of criminal justice has the following main steps:

Step-1: Registration of the First Information Report (FIR).

The process of criminal justice is initiated with the registration of the First Information Report. The FIR is a written document prepared by the police when they receive information about the commission of a cognizable offence.

Step-2: The police officer proceeds to the scene of crime and investigates the facts of the case. Police investigation mainly includes:

- Examination of the scene of crime
- Examination of witnesses and suspects
- Recording of statements
- Conducting searches
- Seizing property
- Collecting fingerprint, footprint and other scientific evidence
- Consulting records and making entries in the prescribed records, like case diary, daily diary, station diary, etc.
- Making arrests and detentions
- Interrogation of the accused

Step-3: After completion of investigation, the officer in charge of the police station sends a report to the area magistrate. The report sent by the investigating officer is in the form of a charge sheet, if there is sufficient evidence to prosecute the accused. If sufficient evidence is not available, such a report is called the final report.

Step-4: On receiving the charge sheet, the court takes cognizance and initiates the trial of the case.

Step-5: The charges are framed. The procedure requires the prosecution to prove the charges against the accused beyond a shadow of doubt. The accused is given full opportunity to defend himself.

Step-6: If the trial ends in conviction, the court may award any of the following punishments:

- Fine
- Forfeiture of property
- Simple imprisonment
- Rigorous imprisonment
- Imprisonment for life
- Death sentence

Courts

The Judiciary has the Supreme Court at the apex having three fold jurisdiction namely, original[3], appellate[4] and advisory[5]. Below the Supreme Court are the High Courts at state level, followed by subordinate courts in the districts. The judiciary in the state functions under the supervision of the High Court[6]. The Constitution empowers the High Courts to issue directions, orders or writs for the enforcement of fundamental rights and for any other purpose[7].

LEVEL OF JUDICIAL AUTHORITY

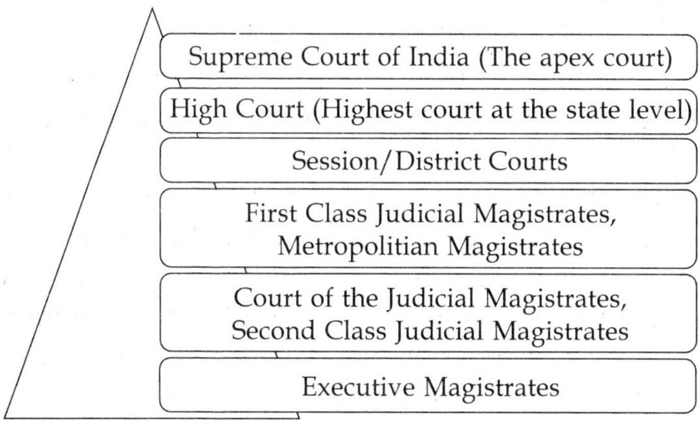

(Note: Session Courts – The courts of session exercise both original and appellate jurisdiction. Major offences like murder, dacoity, robbery, rape etc cannot be tried in a court below the sessions.)

One of the Directive Principles of the state policy laid down in the Constitution required the State to separate judiciary from the executive[8]. This separation was effected through the revised Code of Criminal Procedure in 1974 with regard to criminal justice. It also effected the separation of the prosecuting agency from the police. Prior to this the prosecuting officers at the district level used to function more or less as part and parcel of the district police set-up.

Centre's Role in Policing

Though the Constitution of India has mandated 'Police' and 'Public Order' to be State subjects, there are certain provisions in the Constitution, which empower the Central Government to intervene in some situations or perform special functions in police matters. It is the duty of the Centre to protect the states against internal disturbances and to ensure that the governance of every state is carried on in accordance with the provisions of the Constitution (Article 355).

As per List 1 of the 7th Schedule, the Parliament has exclusive powers to make laws with respect to: *(a)* the armed forces of the Union, which includes the Central Paramilitary Forces (CPMFs) (Entry 2A); *(b)* the Central Bureau of Investigation (CBI) and Intelligence Bureau (IB); *(c)* the Union agencies and institutions for training of police officers, promotion of special studies or research, scientific and technical assistance in the investigation or detection of crime; *(d)* all-India Services; and *(e)* extension of the powers and jurisdiction of members of one state police force to another with the consent of that state or to outside railway areas.

Role of the Ministry of Home Affairs

The Department of internal security, ministry of home affairs, Government of India is responsible for the internal security of the country as a whole. It deals with the Indian Police Service, Central Police Forces, internal security and law and order, insurgency, terrorism, naxalism, activities of inimical foreign agencies, rehabilitation, grant of visa and other immigration matters, security clearances, etc. It performs the following duties in matters concerning police: *(a)* recruiting and managing the Indian Police Service; *(b)* operating the Intelligence Bureau (IB), the Central Bureau of Investigation (CBI) and other Central Police Organisations; *(c)* raising, maintaining and deploying Central paramilitary forces to assist the civil police; *(d)* maintaining a Directorate of Coordination of Police Wireless to provide an independent channel of communication to police forces in the country and a National Crime Records Bureau (NCRB) to ensure computerisation of police forces; *(e)* establishing and maintaining institutions for research, training and rendering of scientific aids to investigation; *(f)* enacting laws for the functioning of the criminal justice system in the country; *(g)* rendering advice and assistance to the state governments in dealing with crime, law and order and other related matters; *(h)* coordinating the activities of various state police organizations; and *(i)* providing financial assistance for the modernisation of state police forces.

Police Divisions

There are two divisions under the Department of internal security:

Police-I: functions as the cadre controlling authority in respect of Indian Police Service (IPS) and also deals with all matters relating to training of police personnel, award of Presidents' Police Medals for meritorious/ distinguished service and gallantry, etc.

Police-II: deals with all matters relating to Central Police Forces, including their deployment.

Endnotes

1. Local Law is applicable to a specific area/jurisdiction and Special Law is applicable to a particular subject.
2. The First Schedule of CrPC lists all offences in the IPC and mentions whether they are cognizable (255 of the offences) or non-cognizable (122 of the offences).
3. The original jurisdiction of the Supreme Court is over disputes between the centre and states and between two or more states, provided the dispute involves any question on which the existence or extent of a legal right depends. Article 32 of the Constitution gives it the power to issue directions/orders/writs for the enforcement of fundamental rights.
4. The appellate jurisdiction of the Supreme Court covers constitutional, civil and criminal cases. In criminal matters, an appeal lies to the Supreme Court from any judgement or order of the High Court if the latter *(a)* has on appeal reversed an order of acquittal and sentenced the accused to death or imprisonment for life or for a period of not less than 10 years; or *(b)* has withdrawn for trial before itself any case and has in such trial sentenced the accused person to death; *(c)* certified that the case is fit for appeal. In any case, the Supreme Court, under Article 136 of the Constitution, can grant special leave to appeal from any

judgement, decree, determination, sentence or order in any matter passed or made by any court or tribunal in the territory of India.

5. The consultative jurisdiction of the Supreme Court is in respect of matters, which are referred for its opinion and advice by the President of India under Article 143 of the Constitution.
6. Article 226 of the Constitution.
7. Article 227 of the Constitution.
8. Article 50 of the Constitution.

2

Combating Terrorism

Role of Village Defence Committees and Special Police Officers

Kuldeep Khoda, IPS*

THE STATE of Jammu & Kashmir has been facing the brunt of terrorism for over two decades. In mid-nineties cross-border terrorism had spread beyond the valley of Kashmir to Doda and other districts in Jammu province. Initial killing of some members of minority community resulted in migration of minority community from remote areas of district Doda. Since it was not possible for the government to provide security in each and every village, particularly in remote areas, an idea was mooted in the year 1995 when I was posted as DIG Doda-Udhampur Range for creation of Village Defence Committees (VDCs) in remote areas of districts of Doda and Udhampur.

* The writer is Director-General of Police (DGP), Jammu & Kashmir.

The idea behind creation of VDCs was to organize a small group of volunteer armed civilians in the identified villages for providing security to their villages, infrastructural installations in and around the village and to check the trans-village movement of terrorists. Towards this end the local volunteers were provided weapons (.303 Rifles) and elementary training for handling of weapons so that, if attacked by terrorists, the volunteers could act in self defence till the time help from nearest security picket could come. As the formation of VDCs in the districts of Doda and Udhampur gained momentum, the migration of minorities which had become quite frequent, particularly in Bhaderwah area of District Doda, dropped sharply initially and later on totally stopped. The incidents of terrorist violence in the villages where VDCs were set up declined noticeably. This experience of community policing had started paying rich dividends. The VDCs have effectively denied the Pakistan-trained militants and foreign mercenaries safe passage to the high mountains and reduced the number of attacks against the minority in far-flung areas.

Initially 660 VDCs were created by the government and the scheme was implemented from 01-10-1995. Keeping in view the outstanding performance of VDCs in combating terrorism in remote areas, the government enhanced the number of VDCs from time to time and at present there are 5000 VDCs sanctioned and operating in the State. This defensive network of volunteer force based on the principle of community policing is expected to grow further. From a scheme launched in 1995 to arm the villagers to ward off increasing militancy, the VDCs have now emerged as an organized fighting arm of the State and a major deterrent to the wanton killing of minorities. It will

not be out of place to mention here that so far 130 VDC members have laid down their lives while fighting against the terrorists. Despite lack of proper training and sophisticated arms, Village Defence Committees have proved invaluable in contributing to normalcy in the State. Success of this effort is a manifestation of the will of the people to actively participate in the fight against militancy.

In the wake of encouraging results from the experience of positioning of VDCs in certain militancy infested areas of the State, an idea to have some kind of an arrangement of placing local youth with the state police/paramilitary forces to help them in combating militancy in their respective areas was developed. With this idea in mind I had, as IGP Jammu Zone, mooted a proposal in early 1997 to have a force of "Special Police Officers" (SPOs) to be selected from local able-bodied youngsters who have aptitude for anti-militancy work and restoration of peace in their area. The aim of forming this force was also to supplement the ongoing efforts of the security forces in dealing with militancy and also in providing valuable information to the security forces regarding movement of militants in their respective areas.

The proposal was discussed at government level and after considering the proposal and visualizing gravity of the ground situation, sanction to the creation of 300 posts of SPOs in each of the four districts of Poonch, Rajouri, Doda and Udhampur in Jammu province was accorded in mid-1997. Local youngsters with aptitude were checked on spot and enrolled as SPOs and after giving them a short training course were put on operational work against terrorists.

Assisting police force/para- military forces in undertaking independent and joint counter terrorist operations was the mainstay of the duties of SPOs. Attuned to the local ethos and ground situation, the engagement of SPOs has been highly result oriented and purposeful. They have been contributing to the best of their capabilities in their job concerning law and order, collecting and developing local intelligence, providing contingency response to meet unforeseen situations and assisting police and other paramilitary forces in undertaking independent and joint anti-terrorist operations. The performance of SPOs has all along been commendable on the anti-militancy front and has also proved to be the backup support base to the Village Defence Committees. SPOs have been coming forward with specific and actionable intelligence inputs. Garnering locally, these inputs collected by SPOs are by and large result oriented. They have rendered selfless and unforgettable share of service in the war against terrorism. Presently, the strength of the SPOs has risen to more than thirty thousand. The achievements of SPOs in anti-terrorist operations have not gone without paying a price and so far 464 SPOs have achieved martyrdom while fighting terrorists. The commendable role of SPOs and VDCs has been highly acknowledged across the board by all those who have been keenly following the events in the Jammu & Kashmir State.

3

Left Wing Extremism in India

ML Kumawat, IPS*

THE SPREAD OF LEFT WING EXTREMISM in a large swathe of India –223 Districts in 20 States–is a matter of serious concern for our democracy. The growing Maoist influence portends an ominous trend. The situation in Chhattisgarh, Jharkhand, Orissa, Bihar, West Bengal and a part of Maharashtra is grim. The death toll of security force personnel due to the Maoist violence in the current year (more than 280 till Nov 2009) is at an all time high.

* The writer retired as Director General of Border Security Force (BSF). He has also been Special Secretary (Internal Security), Ministry of Home Affairs, Government of India and Joint Director - Central Bureau of Investigation (CBI).

TRENDS IN NAXALITE VIOLENCE

Trends in Naxalite Violence						
	2003	2004	2005	2006	2007	2008
No of Incidents	1597	1533	1608	1509	1565	1591
No of casualties in civilians	410	466	524	521	460	490
No of casualties in Security Forces	105	100	153	157	236	231
No of Naxalities killed	216	87	225	274	141	199

Source : MHA Status Report on Naxal violence

It is no wonder then that the Prime Minister, at a recent conference, reiterated, "It would not be an exaggeration to say that the problem of Naxalism is the single biggest internal security challenge ever faced by our country".

A Historical Perspective

The launch of the Communist Party in India in 1925 ushered in a new radical political philosophy which talked in terms of class struggle, revolution and rule of proletariat. By emphasizing problems of land and labour, the party attracted peasants and workers into its fold. It managed to organize big strikes during 1927-29. However, the path of revolutionary armed struggle was put into practice by the Party for the first time in the Telengana region, then a part of Hyderabad Kingdom.

The peasants in Telangana were reeling under the oppressive feudal system. Feudal exaction, bonded labour, high rents and low wages created great discontent among them. The peasants of Telangana guided by the Communists launched their armed struggle in 1946 on economic and agrarian issues such as the abolition of forced labour, redistribution of land, debt relief, grain tax, etc. Within two years the movement gained control of about 3,000 villages and its influence spread to many more although it had to pay a heavy price in terms of 2,000 deaths.

The Communists faced a major dilemma following the surrender of the Nizam to Government of India in September 1948. It was not able to decide whether to call off the movement or to continue it. The majority view prevailed and the movement continued till October, 1951 when the Indian Army's law enforcement measures combined with severe differences of opinion in the Communist Party of India led to the withdrawal of the movement.

The Communists made heavy sacrifices in the movement. P. Sundarayya, a prominent Communist Leader estimates that 4,000 Communists and peasant militants were killed. The 50,000 Armed personnel were deployed by the Government of India to deal with the movement.

The Telangana movement has become a major landmark in the history of Left Wing Extremism in India. B.N Mullik, former Director, Intelligence Bureau, who dealt with the movement summed up its significance: "Telangana remains a great memory and inspiration to the Communist Party of India just as the unsuccessful French Communes have remained an inspiration to the European Communists from the middle of the nineteenth century. If the Communists take to violence again in future, Telangana may very well be the path they follow".

The second Left Extremist movement in India known as Naxalite Movement originated in Naxalbari area of West Bengal in 1967. There the Communists organized tribals of the area on a whole range of agrarian and economic issues such as eviction of tribals, burden of debt, excessive rate of interest on borrowed money, the refusal of landlords to return mortgaged land after the expiry of stipulated period and similar other issues.

A group of tribal peasants under the leadership of the local unit of the CPI(M) had taken control of that area and was propagating the seizure of power over the whole country through armed struggle. The first clash took place between peasants and landed interests on 22 May 1967 when a landlord attempted to forcibly evict a poor tenant from his land in defiance of a court order. The next took place on 23 May when a Police party led by an Inspector was ambushed by a group of rebels armed with bows and arrows resulting in death of the Inspector. On 25 May several Kisan processions went from different parts of Naxalbari and converged on the village Prasadjote. When they held a meeting defying police order, the Sub-divisional Officer of Siliguri ordered the Police to open fire. In the twenty five rounds of firing ten processionists were killed including seven women and two children. It was this incident which got national publicity and associated the whole movement with Naxalbari.

The Maoists who led the Naxalbari uprising described themselves as revolutionaries within the CPI(M). In May 1968, the All India Coordination Committee of Communist Revolutionaries (AICCCR) of CPI(M) was formed which later converted itself in the Communist Party of India (Marxist-Leninist) on 22 April, 1969.

Besides West Bengal, the movement spread to Kerala, Andhra Pradesh, Punjab and many other states. In West Bengal, Calcutta became the centre of Maoist activities. However, the firm handling of Naxalite movement in West Bengal and Kerala coupled with progressive land reforms of far-reaching consequences not only brought the movement under control but these measures prevented its revival in a big way after 1972. The promulgation of emergency in 1975 gave further setback to the Naxalite movement. The post 1972 period till 1986 in Naxalite movement is, therefore, marked by stagnation and low activity.

A notable development in the post-emergency period was the birth and phenomenal growth of the People's War Group (PWG) in Andhra Pradesh. The group, ever since its inception, has dominated the centre stage of Naxalite movement in AP and in its bordering States. The PWG combined its vigorous mass activity with increased militancy and converted north Telangana districts into hunting grounds of Naxalites.

The Recent Resurgence

In the current decade, the Left Wing Extremism has picked up momentum after 2004, with the merger of the People's War Group (PWG) and Maoist Communist Centre (MCC) of Bihar, both in terms of incidence of violence and also in the incremental growth in open activities aimed at mass mobilization. The CPI (Maoist) has been responsible not only for most of the extremist violence but also for the most sensational and audacious attacks against the state.

The Maoists, besides resorting to killings of security forces have resorted to attacks on targets such as railway stations, telephone exchanges, microwave towers, railway tracks, burning of road transport corporation buses, government offices, banks and police stations. These acts of extremists, besides exposing the vulnerability of the state, have given wide publicity to the Maoists.

The overall result of the use of sophisticated weapons, explosives and a new strategy of mobile warfare by the Maoists have resulted in the deaths of a large number of security force personnel, especially in the current year.

MAJOR MAOIST INCIDENTS 2004-2009	
February 2004	Attack on district HQ town of Koraput in Orissa. In a well coordinated and multi-pronged attacks on 13 locations (district Police HQ, district armoury, district treasury, district jail, State Armed Police Battalion HQ and several police stations) 528 service weapons were located.
7 April 2004	28 Policemen killed and 11 injured in landmine blast at West Singhbhum in Jharkhand.
13 November 2005	Hundred of Maoists raided district jail in Jehanabad and freed Maoist cadres and looted 16 weapons.
15 March 2007	Raided a Police Post at Ranibodili, Chhattisgarh and massacred 56 security personnel (including 35 SPOs).
15 February 2008	Large scale attack on Nayagarh town in Orissa. Overran the district armoury, a training centre and a police station, killed 13 policemen and 2 civilians and decamped with 1,100 weapons.
29 June 2008	39 Greyhounds personnel killed as their boat was ambushed and sunk in Orissa.
October 2009	34 Policemen killed in two ambushes in Gadchiroli district of Maharastra.

Open activities of PWG for mobilization of masses are carried out through its large numbered front organizations, which include NGOs, Public Trusts, and various political outfits. These front organizations have widened the base of the Naxalite movement.

Need for Confidence Building

One of the reasons why the Maoist menace has aggravated is because the state hasn't been able to build confidence among the people of these regions. The importance of psychological operations in counter-insurgency cannot be overemphasized. The Maoists too exert great efforts to win the hearts and minds of the tribals and dalits by oral and written propaganda. The state, which is a liberal democratic republic, must mobilize its resources in this field to explain its various programmes and achievements to the people and must be able to effectively communicate the perverseness of the ultimate agenda of the Maoists. The local administrations must pull up their socks and become effective in working for the people. This would be the single most important challenge in order to win back the support of those with grievances. The government must work towards the goal of confidence building among the masses.

Several intellectuals and human rights activists, including a few Gandhians, make outrageous allegations against the security forces. In a recent interview, Himanshu Kumar, a Gandhian, told the *Time of India* (13 Nov ' 09),

"Every day, your forces (referring to the police and para-military forces) demand liquor, chicken, women..., they behead a child in front of his grandfather, rape Adivasi women at will ... And when the Adivasis pick up a lathi, they cry foul. Why are the forces there in Bastar? ... When the police, the administration, the Judiciary have turned against the Adivasis, the Maoists have stood by them. The forces are there only to hunt the tribals from their land, so that the state can hand it over to corporations, the state has no desire for peace and is too arrogant to acknowledge its crimes. We have tried to file 1000 FIR against the Police; not one has been registered. Salwa Judum saw a 22 fold increase in Maoist numbers. Green Hunt will result in genocide of Adivasis. Those who survive will become Naxalites".

Arundhati Roy, a renowned writer, also portrays Maoist as the saviours of tribals when she says,

"Right now in India, the Maoists and the various Marxist-Leninist groups are leading the fight against immense injustice here. They are fighting not just the state, but feudal landlords and their militias. They are the only people who are making a dent. And I admire that". (Source: *The Shape of the Beast;* Penguin)

Yet another celebrated author Mahashweta Devi, when asked in the wake of Jhanabad jailbreak of 2005, said she supported the Naxals. She explained,

"The Naxalites are fighting for Adivasis and weaker sections of people. This fight for the poor is called 'Uggravad' (extremism) by those who lost the support of these poor people, but I call it a 'movement'. Whether these (the Naxal) are CPI(ML) or Naxalites, I want to pay my 'Salam' (salute) at this (old) age to Naxals who are fighting for the poor people. (*Jansatta,* 20 Nov' 2005).

Such strong insinuations coming from opinion makers need to be challenged without fail as their statements and views are read by millions of people. Today, there are a few films in the pipeline that glorify Naxals. One can imagine the adverse impact of such films on impressionable minds.

Intellectuals and social workers remain unaware of the damage such statements might cause to the people themselves by strengthening the Maoists. While human right violations must be pointed out and must be dealt with comprehensively, the cynicism and criticism of some sections is counter-productive to a liberal democracy, however imperfect, and to the very people who such individuals pose to "give voice to". Before it is pointed out that the human rights violations are itself greater threats to democracy, let it be mentioned that the human right violations that do take place are not in the designs and objectives of the state and are not systematic. Rather, they are the exploits of a fringe within the security forces, who the state itself intends to weed out and ensure justice is served. On the other hand, the human rights violations by the Maoists are ignored by these intellectuals and workers; violations that go unchallenged by the Maoist 'system'.

Non-rebuttal of such diatribe may be construed by the people as acceptance of the charges. The government must give utmost importance to perception-management. Such intellectuals and activists must be brought on board by explaining the perils of a possible success by Naxalites. The Government efforts towards the same can be multifold. Apart from debating them publicly, genuine efforts must be made to address their concerns, and where need be, fallacious claims must be refuted. In fact, every comment made by anyone that supports the anti-democracy activities of the Naxals or comments that unfairly condemns the government or forces must be refuted by the government and its several departments, even if this means holding press conferences every day. Perception management is the key because such intellectual support works against our democracy, helping the Naxals while still leaving the hapless tribals in the lurch.

Violent and Disruptive Activities

Today, the threat to national security is greater from internal forces than from external agencies. The Naxalties themselves are not secessionist but they openly support secessionist forces working in our country in the States of J&K, Assam, Nagaland and Manipur, apart from openly supporting anti-Indian Jihadi groups. The Naxalites accused the Government of India that, in the name of "National Integration" these enemies (in the Govt. of India) of the people have been suppressing the genuine rights of all the nationalities and national and religious minorities. The right of self determination is being denied to Kashmiris, Nagas and Mizos.[1] The commonality of interests between the Maoists and secessionist groups in the country portends a serious threat to the internal security of India.

Besides the nexus with the disruptive forces, the Maoists on account of their unabated acts of violence against the people and public properties, such as Banks, Telephone Exchanges, Micro-wave towers,

Roads, Transport Corporation buses, trains, Govt. buildings, bridges etc have caused colossal losses that the people can ill afford.

The Maoists, in their urban perspective plan, describe their intention to 'blow up ammunition depots, destroy communications networks, damage oil installations, etc'. Further, their plan includes the use of cyber warfare for 'damaging the military and other networks'. This can hardly be the objective of groups that are pro-people. Infiltration into the military, para-military forces, police and higher levels of the administrative machinery of the state' to incite revolt is their stated objective.

Need for a Multi-pronged Strategy

The Naxalites movement has survived for over four decades. Its area of influence is now much larger than it was during the first phase of the movement during 1967-72. The movement has retained its appeal to tribals and dalits. There is also some support from the professional groups such as journalists, academics and lawyers as well as civil liberty activists. The state has not succeeded in containing the movement. On the contrary, the movement has shown tremendous grit and determination for survival and has spread to new areas.

The Maoist challenge is complex and formidable. It cannot be contained by security measures alone. The state must follow a multi-pronged strategy. While the armed Maoists will have to be subdued by the Security Forces, the state must work with commitment and missionary zeal to win back hearts and minds of tribals and dalits who provide support to the Maoist. Only inclusive growth where tribals are made partners in the development paradigm will stem the tide. Finally, the human rights activists and radical section of civil society who support the Naxals must be engaged by the state in intellectual debates and convince them that despite all the shortcomings, it is a Democratic Republic alone which can redress problems of tribals and Dalits and teeming millions with freedom and liberty and equality and not the warped and failed ideology which talks in terms of armed insurrection and violence which has been junked even in the country of its origin.

4

Tackling Terror

A Formidable Challenge for Police in India

Dr Nazrul Islam, IPS*

AFTER THE RECENT TERROR ATTACKS, there was much discussion about the challenge of tackling terror by police. Some suggested tougher anti-terror laws like TADA and POTA. Some pleaded for enforcement that is more stringent. Some advocated the creation of a newer terror-tackling agency like the US Department of Homeland Security[1] for deciding the right course of action; we must understand first what terror is.

Terror

Terror is an act of instilling extreme fear in the target group by the use of violence, or threat of use of

* The writer is presently with the Ministry of Railways, Government of India.

violence,[2] to compel them to do certain things, which in normal circumstances they will not do.[3]

Though there are hundreds of definitions of terror,[4] violence is its core. The phenomenon of terrorism can be defined as a strategy whereby violence is used to produce certain effects in a group of people to attain some political ends.[5]

According to UN ad hoc Committee on International Terrorism, it is an heinous act of barbarism committed in the territory of a third state by a foreigner against a person possessing a nationality other than that of the offender for the purpose of exerting pressure in a conflict not internal in nature.[6]

Because of the influential media propaganda of the powerful West, the act of violence by the stronger against the weaker is not termed terror. Only the guerrilla attack of the weaker against the stronger is terror. The mass-scale use of violence by Hitler, Stalin and Bush on the people of Germany, USSR, and Iraq respectively is not terror. The suicide attack by the Iraqi people against the US occupation is, of course, terror. Similarly, the 2002 post-Godhra Gujarat riots, in which about three thousand people were killed, was variously referred to as killing, carnage, mayhem; not as terror. The attack on Akshradham temple on 24 September 2002 was termed terror.

Types of Terror

The major terror-groups operating in India may be classified into a few broad types: nationalist secessionist, religious secessionist, right-wing, left-wing, ethnic, and foreign.

Many people of Kashmir, under organizations like JKLF, want their area to be an independent state. We call them secessionists. They claim themselves nationalist self-determinists[7]. Pakistan is occupying a portion of Kashmir. The rest is in India, as per the accession on 26 October 1947. They cannot fight the military might of India or Pakistan. They resort to guerrilla warfare. Majorities of them are Muslims. Many Muslims of neighbouring Muslim countries are their sympathizers. They get their moral and even logistic support from across the border.

The Khalistani agitation, under organizations like Dal Khalsa, started for making the Punjab a religious state of Khalistan. Their followers in the forces assassinated Prime Minister Indira Gandhi, as she had sent force to the Golden Temple.

The majorities of terror attacks in India are the right-wing Jihadist terror attacks of the so-called Mujahideen groups. There was Hindu-Muslim confrontation in British period. Partition further fuelled it. Muslims are much backward in education and economic conditions. Their representation in the government service is much lower than their percentage. In West Bengal, Muslims are 25.25 per cent of population and only 2.1 per cent of government servants.[8] Some Muslims perceive these because of bias and discrimination of the Hindu-dominated administration. These are so obvious that, in a metro stricken with terror, even a reputed journalist of a leading national daily feels that "the heaviness of a Muslim name could make life miserable".[9] The organizations like HuJI, SIMI, IM, LeT, JeM are exploiting these for terror. The attacks by right-wing organizations like Bajrang Dal are also increasing[10].

Left-wing extremists like PWG in AP-Chhattisgarh, MCC in Bihar-Jharkhand, CPI (ML) in West Bengal also known as Naxal from the name of the village Naxalbari in northern Bengal from where they started the ultra-left movement. They work for armed revolution for equal distribution of properties. In places, they had mass support of the poor people, for whom they struggle. The Maoists' success in Nepal encouraged them.

The people in Northeast belong to over 200 tribes of six major ethnic groups and speak more than 400 languages and dialects. Their distinct social, economic, political, and cultural life remained unaffected by Aryan culture. The British allowed them to practice their traditional institutions and customary laws. Their demand for autonomy was mistaken as secession,[11] this led to different insurgencies like ULFA, BLTF, BSF, NDFB, NSCN, and MNF.[12] The GNLF agitation by the Gorkha of the three hill sub-divisions of Darjeeling district of West Bengal for a separate state of Gorkhaland is also ethnic in nature.

Tackling Terror

Attacks by these terror groups have increased manifolds in the recent time. During the eight years of the 21st century, there were 22 major terror attacks[13] in India, as follows:

Date	Place	Dead	Injured
01 October 2008	Agartala	-	76[14]
29 September 2008	Malegaon	4	70
29 September 2008	Modasa	1	10[15]
27 September 2008	Delhi	1	18[16]
13 September 2008	Delhi	20	40
26 July 2008	Ahmedabad	45	161
25 July 2008	Bangalore	2	20
13 May 2008	Jaipur	60	150
23 November 2007	Lucknow, Varanasi, Faizabad Courts	13	40
25 August 2007	Hyderabad	43	70
18 May 2007	Hyderabad Makka Mosque	10	12
19 February 2007	Lahore bound Samjhauta Express	68	24
08 September 2006	Malegaon	38	100
11 July 2006	Mumbai Suburban trains	186	800
14 April 2006	Delhi Jama Masjid	-	14
07 March 2006	Varanasi	28	62
29 October 2005	Delhi	60	200
24 August 2004	Mumbai	6	–
13 March 2003	Mumbai train	11	–
24 September 2002	Gujarat Akshardham Temple	31	–
13 December 2001	Delhi, Indian Parliament	14	–
01 October 2001	Delhi, Kashmere Gate	40	–

Thus, in the last two years, there were 12 major terror attacks resulting in 268 dead. In the first nine months of 2008, there were seven attacks and 134 dead. India has been one of the major victims of terrorism. Senior national leaders including a prime minister, a former army chief and more than fifty thousand people have lost their lives in terrorist violence in India. The attack on India's Parliament of 13 December 2001 and the Legislative Assembly of Jammu & Kashmir thereafter indicate that the scope and scale of terrorist violence is expanding.[17] The situation has come to such a pass that, there is apprehension of terror attack at any time at any place: market place, working place, and even religious place.

No country can tolerate the killing and maiming of thousands of its innocent people, and attacks on its leaders, legislatures, courts, places of worship. Here lies the urgency for tackling terror. For that, the root causes of terror should be addressed.

Root Causes of Terror

Revenge or remedy for a very deep sense of utter injustice to the perpetrators or their community is the very root cause of terror. There was no suicidal terror attack in Iraq before US occupation. The Iraqis bravely fought the US forces but were decisively defeated by the superior military might of the US.[18] The US occupied the country, installed their puppet government and went on exploiting the country's natural resources. The Iraqis are not able to drive them out in open fight. They also cannot accept the occupation. Therefore, they are becoming suicide bombers. For the same cause, most of the terror attackers of India are from the riot-hit areas.

Between 2001 and 2007, over 71 per cent of all communal incidents took places in Gujarat, Karnataka, Maharashtra, Madhya Pradesh and Uttar Pradesh. Of the people killed in these communal incidents an overwhelming 85 per cent were from these states.

There is correlation between the areas from which terrorists are arising and the deep sense of siege and fear that follows communal violence. The fact that in most cases of communal riots, the perpetrators got away scot-free even where they were identified obviously makes matters worse.[19]

The conviction rate of Mumbai's 1993 blasts was over 80 per cent, while in the post-Babri demolition riot it was not even 0.8 per cent.[20] The mother of one of the persons arrested in connection with Ahmedabad blasts was paralyzed as a result of assault on her by the rioters.

The victimization by the administration, the bias in it, and the thoughtless coverage of the media make the matter worse. In December 2007, Aftab Alam Ansari, was picked up from his Kolkata residence by police of UP and WB, suspecting him to be a terrorist. He was 'thoroughly' interrogated, 'mercilessly' beaten, produced in the court, taken in custody, and then to UP. There were wide front-page coverage and prime time broadcasting about his terror activities and terror connections. Ultimately, he was found innocent. He returned from Lucknow Jail after 22 days. Already he had lost his job, his reputation, and became notorious as a terrorist, making the life of him and his relatives miserable.[21]

In the small hours of 01 September 2008, roughly 50 plainclothes persons of ATS woke up Maulana Mahmoodul Hasan Qasmi, a very respectable person in the Muslim ghetto of Mograpada, Andheri, Mumbai. He was from the family of freedom fighters, was a Unani doctor, and was head of the socio-religious organization 'Anjuman Minhajul Rasool'. They began to interrogate him about terror suspect Tauqeer. When he denied any knowledge, they dragged him to his bakery; a few minutes walk from his house. He was not even allowed to wear his pair of slippers and the customary cap. When their search yielded his photograph with several political leaders including the All India President of the party in power in Centre, they left hurriedly with warning of dire consequences, if he speaks out. Though the ATS chief apologized to the residents of Mograpada, especially its much respected cleric, the damage had been done.[22]

There are instances of killing in fake encounters, and booking in wrong cases. Their relatives and friends suffer from a deep sense of siege and fear. Such victims of communal violence, class violence, and governmental injustice are the easy targets to be turned as terrorists.

Cure for Terror

The cure for terror lies in rooting out the root causes of terror. The goal ought to be to root out terrorism from its very source and breeding place.[23] As terror is the violent expression of a very strong feeling of injustice perpetrated to their community, the best way of tackling terror is by winning the hearts and minds of the people. For that a just world order is necessary. The present world order is based on coercion and exploitation. The UNO is an implement in the hands of a few powerful states[24]. The just world order is against the interest of the leaders of the powerful states. If the USA leaves Iraq, it cannot exploit the oil there. Therefore, tackling terror by winning hearts and minds is not foreseeable. Police can only try to stop the terror attacks by timely collecting intelligence, effecting pre-emptive arrests, and booking offenders.

When United Nations first took up the issue of terrorism in 1972, there were two schools of thought. On the one hand, there were those who were primarily interested in addressing the causes of terrorism. On the other hand, there were those who were more concerned with fighting the manifestations of terrorism itself. The second school of thought has become much more prominent over the last three decades. Today, we even hear voices that plead for disregard of causes of terrorism; perhaps for fear that addressing them could somehow justify terrorism and encourage those who engage in acts of violence to continue atrocities.[25]

Formidable Challenge for Police in India

As the just world-order is against the selfish interests of the political bosses of the powerful states, and beyond the ability of our state, the root-causes of terror cannot be cured. However, terror should be tackled. The challenge is formidable.

The political leaders are hypocritical about their condemnation of terror. They condemn as terror the acts of political violence (of whatever variety) against their own countries or those of their allies, while they fail to admit that their own government sponsors actual terrorism. The US is a clear instance of this. While many of its politicians condemn any political violence against the US targets as being terrorist and criminal actions, not worthy of moral respect, the US has sponsored, through its CIA, various terrorist activities including attempted assassination, covert wars etc.[26] We accuse Pakistan for supporting the Jihadist terror here. They accuse us of fomenting Baluch rebels there. This will not stop. However, terror attacks should be prevented. It is formidable.

The seeds of terrorism are planted in the fertile stagnation of cultural fixation.[27] Police has little role in removing cultural fixation. Hence tackling terror is a formidable challenge.

It has become more formidable because the terror attacks have become 'Fourth Generation Warfare' characterized by a lack of definable battlefield, by groups acting not necessarily under the direct control of the foreign government, and by its transitional nature. It does not rely on massed man-power, massed fire-power, or manoeuvre, as in the First, Second and Third Generation Warfare.

Today's terrorist network and the regimes that support them are unencumbered by fixed borders and conventional forces. It is hydra headed and covert. This enemy's hatred for us is rooted, not in disputes between nations, but in religious fanaticism, tribalism, historic envy, and political ideology. It does not confine its attacks to military targets but murders civilians in an effort to demoralize and destroy the will to fight back.[28] Thus, tackling this transitional war without any definable battlefield and definitely identifiable warriors is formidable.

The problem of police is compounded by the fact that, terrorist to one may be the freedom fighter to the other. Persons like Binay, Badal, and Dinesh were terrorists to the British government, but freedom fighters to the Indian mass. Likewise, many terrorists enjoy the support of the masses. This is why, Osama Bin Laden is still at large though US ordered his capture alive or dead after 9/11.[29] Similarly, many terrorists in India also enjoy the sympathy of people. Police should work to isolate them by their cordial contact with public.

Many terror networks operating in India have training, logistic, and launching facilities in our neighbouring countries. Therefore, the government should tighten the border policing by BSF, ITBP, AR, and SSB. It is, of course, formidable; nonetheless, there is no other option.

Police in India is under the political boss, and thus is an implement in the hands of the party in power. The leaders of the party in power have to work under numerous compulsions. They fail to take any radical decisions to root out the causes of terror. Yet police will have to tackle terror attacks.

The problem of police is more compounded by the fact that police is devoid of a credible image. The Report of People's Union for Civil Liberties team under Rajindar Sachar on 1987 Meerut riots, the Report of the J Ranganath Misra Commission on the 1984 Delhi riots, and the Report of the Justice B N Srikrishna

Commission on 1992-93 Mumbai riots have pointed out the communal bias of police. Her own security guards murdered Prime Minister Indira Gandhi. This is why the public is skeptical of even the honest work of police. Already there is a question whether the persons killed and arrested in Batla House encounter were perpetrators or victims of circumstances.[30] Proper training may remove the bias and improve the image.

A Rand Corporation study of 648 terror groups from 1968 to 2006, across the world, showed that:

1. 244 (38 per cent) were active and 404 (62 per cent) had wound up;
2. 43 per cent of the 404 were absorbed in the political process, 40 per cent were finished by policing like surveillance, infiltration, electronics traps, and tracking money trails, and only 7 per cent were finished by force; [31]
3. only 10 per cent ended achieving their objectives;
4. only 32 per cent of the religious terror groups had wound up, none of these after achieving its objective;
5. group with membership of 10,000 or more lasted longer than smaller groups with less than 1,00 members; and
6. a combination of coercion and political action can force them to negotiation and deprive them of popular support.[32]

These findings demonstrated that larger religious terror groups, the most dreaded terror groups in India, are the hardest nuts to crack. Tougher anti-terror laws be passed, but in a democracy like ours, even terrorists cannot be deprived of a fair trial. Multiplicity of agencies and little coordination among these are the major impediments in the fight against terror in India.[33]

Countermeasures

There should be a tougher anti-terror law providing for institutionalized coordination and cooperation among the different Central and State-UT agencies, by some nodal agency, to deal exclusively with terror cases.

Entry No 8 of the Seventh Schedule and Article 355 of the Constitution provide the legal basis for the creation of an investigating agency with pan-Indian jurisdiction."[34] A task force has already been formed.[35]

Armed with enabling law, competent investigating agency, and public support, police can tackle terror by collecting intelligence, organizing pre-emptive checking, very selective arrest, and effective investigation. The recent breakthroughs in Delhi and Mumbai bear testimony to that.[36]

The most important requirement is timely pinpointed information. Not only the traditional intelligence agencies Central IB, RAW and State IB, SB but also the local police and the security agencies like CRPF, BSF, ITBP, AR and SSB should be used for collecting information. Apart from streamlining official agencies, the government must create a people's assembly in every one or two polling booths. Voters in these booths should elect a five-member executive with the authority to oversee the purely local problems. This elemental unit of Panchayati Raj must be given a new and primary level purely local policing. One main function of this primary policing would be to keep watch on new entrants in the locality and any unusual activities being pursued; [37] the local police should keep close contact with them.

Once information is collected, there should be very cautious checking and very selective preventive arrests. Any wrong arrest, even raid, will not only lower the image of police, but also antagonize a section of people. Police should be trained accordingly.

Even after all these, there may be some failures. Police may foil hundred attempts of the terrorists. They may attend hundred hoax calls. That will not get any publicity. However, a single failure of police in preventing terror attack or attending hoax call will get wide adverse publicity. At that time, police should be very cautious in its steps. Almost all the political leaders try to gain political mileage out of it. The opposition leaders often accuse the ruling leaders for their failure and soft peddling of terrorists. The ruling leaders want some visible actions. The police officers, to please the boss, should firmly avoid making administrative encounters, arrests or at least raids right or wrong.

When there is some terror attack, police should investigate the crime skillfully, taking modern scientific aids, and should effect arrest only when they are sure about the involvement. The target of the slaughter and slander of the terror attacks is the people of India, and not the government. The vast majority of Indian people, majority of them Hindus, are committed to peace and secularism. The jihadist terrorists, by provocative attacks, want to enrage the Hindus to attack Muslims, so that they can convert victims of Hindu attacks to the path of terror. They want to create unbridgeable gulf between the Hindus and Muslims;[38] the police should be aware of this nefarious game plan. To get the confidence of the public, police should avoid random searches, arbitrary arrests and fake encounters. A sense of belongingness should be instilled in the people. Such proper policing can make the terrorists understand that terror is not the source of power.[39]

Conclusion

Eradication of terror lies in the removal of its root causes. As the elimination of the root causes of terror is against the interest of the powerful states, tackling terror is a formidable challenge for police in India. Without removing the causes, terror cannot be eradicated. Police will have to tackle it by detecting terrorist activities and preventing terror attacks. Armed with an enabling law, competent agency, and public support, police will be able in tackling terror.

Endnotes

1. Diwakar, India seeks lesson in US terror war: NSA briefed on Homeland Security set up to thwart post-9/11 attacks, *The Times of India*, Kolkata, 29 September 2008, p 6 c 2
2. Dr John Horgan, What is terrorism, *The psychology of terrorism*, Routledge, New York, 2005, p 1
3. Dr Nazrul Islam, *Islam 9/11 and Global Terrorism*, Viva Books, New Delhi, 2005, p 6
4. Phylip Herbst, Talking Terrorism: A Dictionary of the LoadedLanguage of Political Violence, Greenwood Press, Westport, CT, USA, 2003, p 163

5. N Singh, *World Terrorism and New Age Movement,* Routledge, London, 2002, p 1

6. Assaf Hussain, *Political terrorism and the State in the Middle East,* Mansel, London, 1988, p 17

7. Article 1 of *the 'International Covenant on Economic Social and Cultural Rights*' reads, "All peoples have the right of self-determination. By virtue of that right they freely determine their political status and freely pursue their economic, social and cultural development." As per Article 1 of the 'International Covenant on Civil and Political Rights', "The State Parties to the present Covenant... shall promote the realization of the right of self-determination, and shall respect that right, in conformity with the provisions of the Charter of the United Nations". While acceding to these covenants, the Government of India, on 10 April 1979, declared that "The words 'the right of self-determination' appearing in those articles apply only to the peoples under foreign domination and that these words do not apply to sovereign independent States or to a Section of a people or nation which is the essence of national integrity." Lt Col David L Roberts MBE (Retd) & Dr S Subramanian IPS (Retd), Hand Book of International Humanitarian Law and Human Rights Law, The Regional Delegation of the International Committee of the Red Cross, New Delhi, (Year of publication not mentioned), pp 232-73

8. Appendix, A Report on the Social, Economic and Educational Status of the Muslim Community of India by Prime Minister's High Level Committee, New Delhi, 2006, p 370

9. Shahina K K, Agony of plagiarisation, *The Times of India,* Kolkata, 03 October 2008, p 10 c 7

10. Rajeev Despande, Bajrang Dal: The militant face of saffron family? Shadowy outfit assumes role of avenger of Hindu faith, *The Times of India,* Kolkata, 30 September 2008, p 6 c 4

11. Baljit Singh, *Terrorism and India's Security,* Kulwant Kaur (Ed), Global Terrorism: Issues, Dimensions and Options, Kanishka Publishers, New Delhi, 2005, p 171

12. http://www.freelebanon.org/articles/a167.htm, retrieved on 27 September 2008

13. http://economictimes.indiatimes.com/News/Politics Nation/Chronology_of_major_bomb_attacks_in_India/articleshow/303 7346.cms, 28 September 2008, p 1 c 6, retrieved on 28 September 2008
14. Manas Paul, 6 held for Agartala blasts, no fatalities, *The Times of India,* Kolkata, 03 October 2008, p 1, c 2
15. 5 die in twin blasts, *The Statesman,* Kolkata, 30 September 2008, p 1 c 2
16. Fer Bisforan Dillite, Hata 1, *The Rabibarer Dainik Statesman,* Kolkata
17. Baljit Singh, *Terrorism and India's Security, Kulwant Kaur (Ed), Global Terrorism: Issues, Dimensions and Options,* Kanishka Publishers, New Delhi, 2005, p 165
18. In 2002, US Defence Budget was $ 379 billion. US economy accounted for 22 per cent of world output, it led the world in all cutting-edge technologies, its military spending was more than 25 next largest militaries of the world, the military spending of USA along with its allies was more than that of the rest of the world. Ninan Koshy, War on Terror, Left World, New Delhi, 2002, p 6, p 12.
19. Subodh Varma & Rema Nagarajan, Terrorists breed most in riot heat areas: TOI explores whether there is correlation between communal incidents and growth of terrorism, *The Sunday Times of India,* Kolkata, 21 September 2008, p 9 c 1
20. Muhammad Wajihuddin, *The Sunday Times of India,* Kolkata, 21 September 2008, p 7 c 1
21. Siladitya Sen, Aftab Alam Ansari, *Ebang kayekti cinema, The Ananda Bazar Patrika,* 29 September 2008, p 4 c 6
22. Muhammad Wajihuddin, *The Sunday Times of India,* Kolkata, 21 September 2008, p 7 c 1
23. M G Chitkara, *Combating Terrorism,* APH Publishing Corporation, New Delhi, 2003, p 15
24. Dr Nazrul Islam, *Reforming the United Nations,* Viva Books, New Delhi, 2006, pp 23-25
25. Alex P Schmid, *Prevention of terrorism,* Tore Bjorgo (Ed), *Root Causes of Terrorism: Myth, reality and ways forward,* Routledge, New York, 2005, p 223

26. J Angelo Corlett, *Terrorism: A Philosophical analysis*, Kluwer Academic Publishers, Dordrecht, Netherlands, 2003, p 48
27. Don J Feeney Jr, *Creating Cultural Motifs against Terrorism*, Praeger, Westport, CT, USA, 2003, p 31
28. Candace de Russy, *Academy and Fourth Generation Warfare*, David Clarke (Ed), *Technology and Terrorism*, Transaction Publishers, New Brunswick, 2004, p 231
29. Ninan Koshy, *The War on Terror*, Left World, New Delhi, 2002, pp 1-14
30. Kajari Bhattacharya, Victims or Perpetrators? Sanjarpur tells its tale, *The Statesman*, Kolkata, 24 September 2008, p 1 c 2;
31. Political Bureau, Now Congress raises doubt over Delhi encounter, *The Economic Times*, Kolkata, 02 October, 2008, p 2 c 7
32. Subodh Varma, What kills terror? Politics & policing, *The Times of India*, Kolkata, 24 September 2008, p 1 c 7
33. Subodh Varma, Govt action can rob terror group of its mass support, *The Times of India*, Kolkata, 24 September 2008, p 7 c 8
34. Diwakar, India seeks lesson in US terror war: NSA briefed on Homeland Security set up to thwart post-9/11 attacks, *The Times of India*, Kolkata, 29 September 2008, p 6 c 2
35. Sankar Sen, Ominous portents: Stringent law must authorise Central Investigation, *The Statesman*, Kolkata, 30 September 2008, p 6 c 2
36. *The Dainik Statesman*, Kolkata, 09 October 2008, p 5 c 3

    The Times of India, Jaipur, 07 October 2008, p 1 c 2
37. Rajinder Puri, Five-point plan against terror, *The Statesman*, Kolkata, 25 September 2008, p 6 c 2
38. M J Akbar, Tentacles of dread and the terror game plan, *The Sunday Times of India*, Kolkata, 21 September 2008, p 7 c 1
39. Dr Nazrul Islam, *Santras Kshamatar Utsa Nay, Bhasha O Sahitya*, Kolkata, 2008, pp 30-33.

5

Naxalism

Mechanism of Operation and Strategy to Tackle

Dr PK Agrawal, IAS*

NAXALITE PROBLEM is at present India's gravest threat to internal security. To quote Prime Minister Manmohan Singh, not a day passes without an incident of Leftist extremism at some place or the other. Elaborating the alarming network of Naxalite, Ajit Doval, a former director of the Intelligence Bureau (IB) had earlier stated that Naxal activity affects approximately 40 per cent of the country's landmass and at least 35 per cent of the total population. Naxal violence in states like Chhattisgarh, Jharkhand, Orissa, Andhra Pradesh and Bihar has been of late a regular affair. However, what is worrying to

* The writer was Additional Chief Secretary, Government of West Bengal.

the nation is the penetration of its rebels deep into Maharashtra, Karnataka, Uttar Pradesh, and West Bengal, Madhya Pradesh and other states and even UTs.

It has been proved beyond doubt that one of the repercussions of non-implementation of land reforms was responsible for the growth of 'Naxalite' movement. The surfacing of the Naxalite movement in 1966 in West Bengal and its positive ending by the Left Front Government by implementing land reforms measure has proved this case in point very clearly.

The Naxalite movement was an important movement that covered 80 million landless people including 30 million tribal. The political and militant character of Naxal movement arose out of a sense of discontentment and disillusionment against the CPI(M)'s inability and other factors to implement the land reform even after forming the United Front Government in West Bengal in 1976. The Naxalite or the CPI(M-L) introduced a distinct style of peasant warfare, with its distinct ideology and strategy. This movement more than any other, shook the national sense. The government feels its tremors in Andhra Pradesh, Chhattisgarh (Bastar district) and in Jharkhand.

Left Wing Extremism

There are many Left Wing Extremist (LWE) groups operating in the country with lot of underground and overground cadres and supporters. While aiming to establish a classless society based on egalitarian principles and revolutionary struggles, resorting to violence remains the cornerstone of the tactics of most of the major LWE groups. The CPM-People's War Group (53 per cent) and Maoist Communist Centre (MCC) (30 per cent) continue to spearhead LWE violence respectively.

The basic thrust of the different outfits is to focus attention on the grievances of the people, inequities suffered by large segments of the population, release of victims of exploitation from the tentacles of the landlords, etc. and to inculcate 'class' responsibilities among the economically and socially deprived sections. In pursuance of these objectives, the groups have not only mobilized the people but have also ensured that distributive justice is available in a rough and ready manner. The peoples' courts organized by these groups expropriate surplus land from the landowners and distribute it amongst the landless, dispense criminal justice, settle disputes and punish offenders. Thus, 'Jan Adalats' constitute the cornerstone of their efforts to win over the masses, particularly in the rural areas. Besides, they indulge in extortion from businesspersons, contractors, traders, government officers etc. and resort to murders and kidnappings to eliminate interference by agents of the established administration and defiant class enemies.

Various LWE groups have their presence in different parts of the country, notably the heartland states including Andhra Pradesh, Bihar, Jharkhand, Madhya Pradesh, Chhattisgarh, Maharashtra, West Bengal etc. The CPML-PWG is well entrenched in almost all districts of AP, several districts of central and south Bihar, Jharkhand, southern districts of MP, Chhattisgarh and Orissa and a few eastern districts of Maharashtra and three districts of

West Bengal. The most of extremism-affected districts have gone to the newly created state of Chhattisgarh. It also has a presence in a few districts of Karnataka and Tamilnadu.

The movement did not bring any immediate results in West Bengal and was short-lived but had far-reaching implications and became a force behind numerous peasant struggles in different areas of West Bengal, Bihar, Jharkhand, Chhattisgarh (by tribal), Andhra Pradesh and Punjab. However, the Left Front Government led by CPI(M) in its three successive terms starting from 1977 salvaged the situation by recording about fifteen lac sharecroppers known as bargadar under the "Barga operation" programme. Proper distribution of surplus lands to the landless and providing them bank credits consolidated this programme.

So far, the government has given land to about 29 lakh pattaadar. Up to 1978, in six years 74,000 people got crop-finance whereas in the year 1976 alone 59,000 got crop-finance. Thus, the CPM government in West Bengal has consolidated its position, making Central and other state governments envious of them.

Mechanism of Functioning of the Naxalite

Maoist Communist Centre was formed in 1969 after Amulya Sen and Kanai Chatterjee parted company with Charu Mazumdar who believed in annihilating the class enemies. Sen and Chatterjee emphasized on public movement. It is a different story that later on M.C.C. itself got involved in direct action to finish the so-called class enemies. Initially, they indulged into settlement of local dispute by force, threatening big landowners, illegal realization from forest contractors, killing of informers, indulging in arson and looting.

MCC has three frontal organizations, namely, (a) Party organization, (b) Force/army organization and (c) People organization.

The organization has area-wise special committees for Bihar-Bengal, Assam-Tripura, Bihar-Uttar Pradesh, Bengal-Orissa and Andhra Pradesh-Orissa. At various levels the party has corresponding militia organization. It has people's organizations in the names of Revolutionary Farmers Committee, Revolutionary Cultural Organization, Women Liberation Association, Communist Young League, Farmers' Movement Front, Labourers Liberation Organization, Revolutionary Students' League, and Intellectuals Organization etc. from village level to central committee level. There are members and office bearers for each committee or organization.

Similarly, Peoples' War Group (PWG) has organizational set up from central committee, special zonal committee (at the state level), regional committee, divisional committee, area committee and down to the village committee. PWG established this in 1980 and spread its wing mainly in Telangana region of Andhra Pradesh, Orissa, Chhattisgarh, Jharkhand and a few parts of Karnataka. It is a militant organization of the platoon level. The platoon is equipped with latest weaponry and is expert in guerrilla warfare. They have women members who successfully incite public for violence. Two other Naxalite organizations are namely CPI(ML) (Vinod Mishra) and CPI(ML) Party Unity(PU). CPI(ML) (VM) is well equipped with men and arms, yet it believes in taking part in election process.

MCC aims at publicising their ideology so that people in large number may be associated with the party. They want to usurp the movable and immovable properties of the capitalists. On police intervention, they loot the weapons of police force after attacking them. After taking possession of land of big landowners, they allow their members to cultivate those lands and even realize money from the landowners as levy.

Their strategy is to associate local people in their organization and continue warfare with their support, to expose ruling class by describing their luxurious ways of life and to take local populace into confidence before start of the guerrilla warfare. Once they declare any area as guerrilla zone, they administer at the village level through their supporters, by giving armed protection through various armed guerrilla formations.

PWG specially utilize landmines to cause large number of casualties to the police force, which also facilitates them to loot police arms. This is a greater demoralising strategy than the ambush or attack by encircling the police force. Sometimes they come as labourers and sometimes in other disguises. One section engages the sentry of the police outpost whereas the others take position to launch a full-fledged assault. Sometimes they come in disguise at the police station to give sensitive information of Naxalite attack, rape, and then take advantage of the empty police outpost and run away with arms and ammunitions. While they come to attack in a big way on any prison or police station or police lines in a sub-divisional or district headquarter, they forcibly take villagers with them who act as human shield for them. They occupy government vacant land, forest land and benami lands. They do not allow the sale of these lands. They hold people's courts in villages and settle local disputes amicably. They enrol disgruntled unemployed youths by convincing them about the failures of government. They also kidnap officials to pressurize local administration. They burn down roadways, buses, railway stations or telephone centres. They scare away police informers, and contractors by causing explosions nearby. They attack police stations. They call bandh or road blockade to show their strength with a view to participate in the political process ultimately to run their large organizational structure, they extort money from the landowners, moneyed men and the contractors. They execute their action in following four phases:

- identify the area,
- develop contacts with the local people of that area to make them their supporters,
- commit serious offences by forming groups,
- form liberated zones.

In the liberated zones, they run parallel administration and extort money from the contractors and government officials. If the identified person does not pay, they kill him on the spot. They however, continue to strengthen their armoury.

Recruitment

They lure young villagers to come to their fold by offering them monthly remuneration or by giving them financial assistance apart from brainwashing them into their ideology. Sometimes, the people from the oppressed class join these organizations to take revenge from the powerful class who have been harassing and exploiting them so far. Once they join their organization, they have to follow their diction and discipline or drill. If someone violates, they kill him then and there. They strictly follow discipline to respect women and follow the local customs, cultural rituals and local behaviour.

They have their selected training centres, which are generally located in the dense forest. The trainers generally come from Andhra Pradesh. Training periods generally vary from one to two months. After the training, they give him the charge of a centre for a period of six months to a year.

This way, they build up a militarily strong and politically sound organization. Their cadres are physically tough and mentally alert. Thus, the Naxalite build an organization, which can run parallel to the government organization. Apart from regular army training, the cadres have to attend classes for their educational improvement.

Strategy

They do not surrender because Comrade Charu Mazumder said that the surrender was tantamount to committing suicide. Similarly, Comrade Mao said that the attack is the best defence. They adopt three tactics of assault. First is raid, which is resorted to as "hit and run" tactic so that they may create panic in the police force and can run away with their arms and ammunitions and to kill a selected police officer, cruel landowner, middleman or political leader. Second is the attack, which they organize for the release of some important comrades from the police custody or from jails.

Third type is ambush. After ambush, the members of assault group hide themselves within a distance of 50-60 metres so that they can finish their enemies by continuous firing or grenade attack.

As the Naxalite are well aware of the terrain, they take position at such a place that they can see the police force clearly, whereas the police or paramilitary force cannot see them clearly, as the latter is equipped with more sophisticated arms like LMG, machine gun, grenades, etc.

The Naxal groups are experts in laying the mines as the area is in their control. The village roads are not pucca. It is where the most powerful police or paramilitary force is scared of these extremist groups. Even use of helicopters cannot help them to locate the extremist's groups because they go under the forest or cave corner. They also use dresses like army or paramilitary force, which merge with the background of their terrain. Over and above, local informers are always there for their assistance whether for fear or for reasons of ideological oneness. This is why the most powerful police forces of Tamilnadu and Karnataka could kill Veerappan only after decades of chase.

Sources of their Income

- Realising ransom after kidnapping of government officials or local rich people.

- Realising money after forcibly occupying lands of rich landowners.
- Realising subscription for the PT in the morning and drill in the evening.
- Realizing proceeds by giving forest or government lands on lease.
- Realizing levy from rich persons and traders.
- Selling forest or mineral produce lying in government stockyard.
- Realizing levy from government officials and officers.
- Their expenditures are well regulated. They keep the accounts of each rupee. If one indulges in dishonesty, they finish him off. Thus, corruption has not yet crept into Naxal organizations they are operating on the same Indian soil. Their life-style is also simple. Leaders and cadres lead same type of simple living.
- As per police reports, vices of drinking, gambling, sex-exploitation, comfortable life style are also afflicting the Naxal organizations. They have four hours of physical training and have classes for three hours before lunch and two hours at night. With such brainwashing, no cadre likes to come out of the Naxal outfit.

There are magazines like *Lai Pataka, Lal Chingari, Krantikari Geetmala, Bigul Masik Samachar, Jan Jwar,* and *Struggling Forum* for people's resistance. They publish these magazines regularly. They carry out their activities not only in India but foreign countries like Nepal, Philippine, Peru etc. as well.

The focus of their leadership is on police atrocities to keep their cadres on boil to strike on the police force to an unusual extent.

They ultimately want to bring bloody revolution on Mao Zedong paradigm. They start by advocating the cases of landless peasantry. Ultimately, their main aim is diluted and one sees an all-round struggle for land and basic facilities in the villages. If the government meets their legitimate demands, the Naxal will not be able to muster strong support from the common people. Thus, it is high time to understand the Naxalite strategy and their genuine demands. If they do not come to terms, they cannot defeat the well-armed mighty state of India.

Naxal believe in the ideology of Mao and Marx. Allegedly, the Naxalites receive foreign assistance. However, their main aim was and is agrarian, to distribute land among the landless. In pursuance of that, they mobilize poor peasants. They want to establish or seize power in their base areas. Thus, they are also very clear that unlike success of Naxalism in a small country like Nepal, they cannot seize political power in small states, let alone the whole country. For the time being their violent campaign in small states like Chhattisgarh and Jharkhand will be successful but when the government deploys security forces across the country, they will be helpless. Central Government and state governments are raising lakh of armed soldiers to fight a combined Naxal force of not more than 12,000 personnel. In fact, the Naxalite movement is diffusing though the Naxal are not as sophisticated and well equipped as the police forces are. It is because of their exalted aim to ensure right of cultivation to the rural poor. They perpetuate violence to achieve their agrarian aim. However, on many an occasion the movement fails because it is not a scientifically led movement or force.

The armed struggles began in Naxalbari in North Bengal with the avowed aim to obtain the rights of the agricultural labour in tea gardens by enabling them to become owners of the land that they had been cultivating for the powerful and established tea garden owners. With the objective of making the exploited cultivators the owners of the land on which they work, this movement diffused from the coastal plains of Srikakulam in Andhra Pradesh to Sonbhadra in Uttar Pradesh and from the Santhal Parganas in Jharkhand to Dantewala in Chhattisgarh. According to a report of the Social Council for Social Development, this armed struggle has spread to 170 of the total 607 districts in the country. This means that the law and order situation in one fourth of the country has touched a new low. The Central Government has spent crores of rupees to tackle the problem of Naxalism but the affected governments have not put forward any viable solution to land reforms. It is unfortunate that the affected state governments are insensitive to the sensitive issue of land reforms. Nevertheless, their ears are oversensitive to the gunfire. For example, since the creation of the state of Chhattisgarh in 2000, the state government has made no voluntary effort for restoring or distributing land to its landless tribal. In 2003, after a prolonged movement by a people's organization in Kanwardhah district of Chhattisgarh, the government announced distribution of land to 6,100 families of the Baiga tribe but they have achieved only 40 per cent of their self-fixed target. On the other hand, the Chhattisgarh government acquired in the last six years an estimated 42,000 acres of and for industrial purpose in the tribal dominated districts of Sarguja, Kanwardhah and Raigadh.

Land acquisition is a new weapon in the hands of Naxal organizations. It is a fact that police forces are quick to arrest their theoreticians, thinkers, guides, moral supporters from the urban hideouts but this hardly affects the Naxalite outfits in far-flung forests living with people's support. The Indians are peace loving. In addition, the Indian farmers are yet more peace loving. Therefore, the Naxalite movement will not lose its support base until tangible benefits reach the local people. The people even in Jammu and Kashmir are fed up with consistent incidents of violence. Sometimes, they also lose their kith and kin in crossfiring. They have to part with their paltry food items to the volunteers or cadres of Naxalite. Thirdly, sometimes Naxal or the police force exploits their women. This exploitation by the Naxal or security forces is a reason in the chain of reasons that impels the populace to return to the peaceful democratic society, corruption, nepotism and inefficiency of the system not with standing far more tolerable than the constant gun fire or bloodshed.

As a result, the Naxalite movement is fast moving to new areas. Its avowed object is not questionable. But like government policy, its implementation is not possible in practice.

Naxalite are adopting new strategies, and weapons to spread their movement. The Government should also change its strategies from negative to positive so that the Naxalite problem meets its end once for all. They should not view the Naxalite as their enemies or Red terrorists but the ones who have challenged them in their slumber to rise and deliver justice to the rural poor specially the Dalits and the Adivasis.

The villagers are the worst hit in crossfire. A villager has rightly remarked, "Between the government and the Naxalite, the government is a better alternative but till the time a democratic government reaches my village and my doorstep, the Naxalite are definitely preferable". However, the violence and violence, which is order of the day, be brought to an end at all costs.

Strategy to Tackle Naxalism

The present strategy to tackle extremist outfits is a simple fire- fighting mechanism based on police report. There is hardly any input from the radical thinker, civil servants or politicians.

The police organizations furnish so much intelligence information that it leaves no gap or scope to the policy-planners or top executives to think otherwise. Directorate of Intelligence Bureau is one of the best-organized networks in the country. It has a store of readymade information, which emerges from the ground level informer who is not much educated. With the police orientation of his mind for number of years, he cannot think otherwise except to meet violence with violence. Secondly, during his term with the police organization, he has not come across land reform measures being implemented in the field. The very mindset of police is that there is nothing good in the society. Whatever small good they can do, is the only alternative. Through such an apparatus, the information filters and reaches in a very well couched language on the table of the minister through the secretary of the department. Invariably, the secretary will not offer his suggestions for the fear that the police professionals will pooh-pooh his suggestions. The top brass of the police have easy access to the top political executive and they certainly bypass the civil service secretary. Therefore, the path of least resistance for the secretary is to pass the papers as received from the intelligence wing of the police force. Therefore, the home ministry has to design a strategy to meet violence by the state violence, tooth for tooth and an eye for an eye. Ultimately, the government will have to ask the police or paramilitary force to battle with the Naxalite violence. Therefore, the best strategy is to approve a plan of action and provide the security police or paramilitary, whichever force the government decides upon with weapons, they want, to end this menace of Naxalism forever. Some of the conscientious police officers raise dissenting voice, but their voice is not heard and sometimes it is suppressed as theoretical, academic or outdated. Mostly, the civil service officers manage the ministry of home affairs, yet the strategy finalized by them does not show any result whatsoever. Therefore the job of designing the strategy should be given to right people, security force in this case to do the strategizing.

The Naxalite uprising is the most dangerous uprising which has taken an unprecedented toll of human life. The figures from 2003 to 31 October 2006 are set below:

1.	Personnel of police or paramilitary force killed	492
2.	Civilians killed	1876
3.	Naxalite killed/untraceable	736
4.	Incidents	6610
5.	No. of Naxalite arrested	5667
6.	No. of surrendered Naxalite	4890

The question is why the innocent villagers join the extremists. It cannot be that all of them are coerced or blackmailed to join the outfit.

It is a happy sign that of late wisdom has begun to dawn on the mandarins of MoH. The home ministry has asked the rural development department to quicken the pace of development in the far-flung Naxalite-affected areas. The concerned ministry has received urgent requests to implement schemes in the tribal and such scheduled caste regions where exist the majority of Naxalite outfits. However, one fails to understand why the ministry of home affairs is not shelling out funds from its own coffers. The problem is MoH's baby. It should take care of it. Other than raising battalions of paramilitary forces and purchasing sophisticated arms for them, they should earmark a percentage of funds for developmental activities in Naxal affected regions. The response from other departments of Central Government and state government is lukewarm because they do not know how to go about it. The MoH has to educate the development from ministry's babus secretary to a clerk. They must be made to realize that they would not be able to carry out their developmental plans if the district administration at the grassroot remains busy in tackling the Naxalite problem. The district administration implements the developmental work. That is what they should be educated.

Naxal have still not lost faith in civil administration of the district though they have lost faith in election process and in Panchayat bodies because these bodies play partisan role in the rural India. If panchayats execute schemes impartially and honestly, they can tackle the Naxalite problem. The revenue department or land and land reforms department can accomplish the rest of the job. But because of the vested interests or to hide their inefficiency or due to lack of political will, their only agenda is to identify the patta-holders or assignees of vested lands to ensure that real possession of government surplus land goes to them. To say the least, it will take those five years to accomplish this primary task of land reform. Land reform is a continuous never-ending process. It will end only when all the landless become at par with the landowners. This will mark the beginning of an egalitarian rural society.

The Government of India has adopted a strategy, which it circulated to state governments for guidance to bring down the rigour of Naxal violence in the country mainly as security centric measures.

As per the report appearing in *Telegraph* of 23 May 2008[1] the Maoists have widened their network three folds in the past two years, spreading to 183 districts from 55 in 2005 across 16 states, the Centre believes. In fact, fully Naxal affected districts are 76 only in India as on date as per a more specific survey and information submitted to Parliament.

Let us examine what strategy the Central government has adopted and circulated to state governments for guidance to bring down the Naxal violence

The home ministry lists Kerala, Tamilnadu, Punjab, Haryana, Uttarakhand, Uttar Pradesh and Delhi as the states where the Maoists have established new bases by setting up regional and district-level centres. The strength of the armed Maoists cadre too has risen from 8000 in 2005 and 11,000 in 2006 to 15,000 in 2007.

Policy to deal with the Naxalite Menace

The present policy of the Government of India comprises the following components:

- The government will deal sternly with the Naxalite indulging in violence.
- Keeping in view that Naxalism is not merely a law and order problem, the policy of the government is to address this menace simultaneously on political, security, development, and public perception management fronts in a holistic manner.
- Naxalism being an interstate problem, the states will adopt a collective approach and pursue a coordinated response to counter it.
- The states will need to further improve police response and pursue effective and sustained police action against Naxalite and their infrastructure individually and jointly.
- There will be no peace dialogue by the affected states with the Naxal groups unless the latter agree to give up violence through arms.

- Political parties must strengthen their cadre base in Naxal-affected areas to wean away the youth from the path of Naxal ideology.
- The states from where Naxal activity/influence, and not Naxal violence, is reported should have a different approach with special focus on accelerated socio-economic development of the backward areas and regular interaction with NGOs, intelligentsia, civil liberties groups etc. to minimize over ground support for the Naxalite ideology and activity.
- Efforts will continue to promote voluntary local resistance groups against Naxalite but in a manner that the villagers get adequate security cover and the security forces effectively dominate the area.
- To use mass media extensively to highlight the futility of Naxal ideology and violence and loss of life and property caused by it and development schemes of the government in the affected areas to restore people's faith and confidence in the government machinery.
- The states should announce a suitable transfer policy for the Naxal affected districts. The states would need to post willing, committed and competent officers with a stable tenure in the Naxal-affected districts. These officers will also need greater delegation and flexibility to deliver better, step up government presence, and above all improve governance in these areas.
- The Government of Andhra Pradesh has an effective surrender and rehabilitation policy for Naxalite and has produced good results over

the years. The other states should adopt a similar policy.

- The state governments will need to accord a higher priority in their annual plans to ensure faster socio-economic development of the Naxal-affected areas. The target areas should distribute land to the landless poor as part of the speedy implementation of land reforms, ensure development of physical infrastructure like road, communication, power etc. and provideemployment opportunities to the youth in these areas.
- Another related issue is that development activities are nothappening in some of the Naxalite-affected areas mainly due to extortion, threat or fear from the Naxalite cadres. In these areas, even contractors are not coming forward to take up developmental work. The Naxal-affected areas will need additional security and other measures to facilitate un-interrupted developmental activities.
- The Central Government will continue to supplement the efforts and resources of the affected states on both security and development fronts to bring about greater coordination between the states to tackle the problem.

Countermeasures

The counter action by the affected states in terms of Naxalite killed, arrested, surrendered, and arms recovered from them was better during 2005 and 2006. There is an urgent need to improve and strengthen police response particularly by the state of Chhattisgarh, Jharkhand, Bihar, Orissa and Maharashtra by improving actionable intelligence collection, sharing mechanisms and strengthening their police forces on the pattern of SIB and Greyhounds in Andhra Pradesh. Unfortunately, 38 Greyhounds commandoes, while crossing a water body in Malkangiri district of Orissa, died in a Naxalite attack.

Police Response

As requested by the affected states the Centre has deployed paramilitary forces on long-term basis. This is to help the states to provide an effective response to the Naxal violence. The Central Government has also exempted the states from the payment of cost of deployment of these forces for a three-year period from 01 July 2004.

Besides, the Centre has sanctioned India Reserve (IR) battalions for the Naxal-affected states to strengthen the security apparatus at their level to enable them to provide gainful employment for the youth, particularly in the Naxal areas. Recently, the Centre has given the approval for raising ten additional IR battalions for the Naxal-affected states. The Central Government will now provide Rs. 20.75 crores per IR battalion as against the earlier amount of Rs. 13 crores per battalion.

Recruitment in Central Paramilitary Forces

In order to wean away the youth from the path to militancy or Naxalism, recruitment guidelines permit 40 per cent recruitment in Central paramilitary forces from the border areas and areas affected by militancy or Naxalism.

Salva Judum in Bastar Region, Chhattisgarh

Salva Judum, an anti-Naxal movement began in June 2005 in Bastar region of Chhattisgarh as a spontaneous expression of pent-up anti-Naxalite sentiments among the local people. The movement was triggered off by a meeting of eight villages at Teomar village under PS Kutru of police district Bijapur, where the villagers expressed their unhappiness with the modus operandi of Naxalite causing harassment and starvation of common villagers due to cutting off of employment opportunities. Salva Judum activists mobilized villagers/tribal against Naxal through a series of rallies, meetings and padyatras in Naxal strongholds of the two blocks [Bijapur and Bhairamgarh] of Bijapur police district in South Bastar. This voluntary and peaceful movement by local people has now spread Bijapur, Bhairamgarh, Usoor, Sukma and Konta blocks in Dantewada district. So far, Salva Judum activists have held more than 150 anti-Naxalite rallies.

The spread of Salva Judum beyond the Bhairamgarh and Bijapur blocks of Dantewada district, into the West (Usoor block) and the south (Konta and Sukma blocks) of Dantewada district (bordering Andhra Pradesh) seems to have caused a major setback to the CPI (Maoist), who had till recently been enjoying a complete dominance in the area. Naxalite have thus resorted to killing of civilians/tribal to threaten Salva Judum activists with an aim to derail the Salva Judum campaign.

Keeping in view the importance of Salva Judum movement as a major bulwark in sustained campaign against Naxal and in view of the Naxalite attacks on innocent Salva Judum activists, the centre has advised state government to enhance the deployment of security forces to provide effective area domination, ensure safety of Salva Judum activists and strengthen security of relief camps.

Backward Districts Initiative [BDI]

To address the Naxalite menace on the developmental front, the Central Government has provided financial assistance of Rs. 2,475 crores for 55 Naxal-affected districts in nine states. These states are Andhra Pradesh, Bihar, Chhattisgarh, Orissa, Jharkhand, Maharashtra, Madhya Pradesh, Uttar Pradesh and West Bengal. The Centre has given this financial assistance under the Backward Districts Initiative (BDI) component of the Rashtriya Sam Vikas Yojana (RSVY). Each of the districts will receive an amount of Rs. 15 crore per year for three years to fill in critical gaps in physical and social development in the Naxal-affected areas. Apart from these districts, other Naxal-affected areas/districts too will benefit under the Backward Regions Grant Fund (BRGF) Scheme, which covers 250 backward districts in the country and has an outlay of nearly Rs. 4,000 crores from this fiscal year (2006-07) onwards.

Tribal and Forest Related Issues

In order to address the areas of disaffection among the tribal, the government introduced the Scheduled Tribes [Recognition of Forest Rights] Bill 2005, in Parliament on 13 December 2005, which has now become an Act. Further, to facilitate social and physical infrastructure in the forest areas, ministry of environment and forests has issued general approval to allow such infrastructure by utilizing up to 1 hectare of forest land for non-forest purposes. The ministry has also permitted the mending of kutcha roads with metalled road.

Land Reforms and Creation of Employment Opportunities

Naxal groups have often raised land and livelihood related issues. Taking up the land reforms on priority basis and allot the surplus land to the landless and the poor in the Naxal areas will go a long way in tackling the developmental aspects of the Naxal problem. The Centre has asked the states to pay more attention to this task besides accelerating people centric developmental activities and create employment opportunities in the Naxal-affected areas. In addition, the states are to focus on creation of physical infrastructure in terms of roads, communication, power, schools, hospitals, etc.

Monitoring Mechanisms

The Central Government accords high priority to review and monitor the Naxal situation and the measures taken thereof by the states. Several monitoring mechanisms have been set up at the Centre for this purpose. These include a periodical review by the Cabinet Committee on Security (CCS) of the Naxal situation, a Standing Committee of the chief ministers of the Naxal-affected states. The latter is chaired by the Union home minister. The Union home secretary chairs the quarterly coordination meetings with the chief secretaries and the directors general of police of the affected states. The special secretary (IS), MHA presides over the monthly task force meetings of nodal officers of Naxal-affected states and Central agencies. The states have the standing instruction to hold a monthly review by the DGP and a bi-monthly review by the chief secretary on the Naxal situation and the measures and strategies taken to contain the Naxal problem on both security and development fronts.

Meeting of the Standing Committee of Chief Ministers of Naxal Affected States

The Standing Committee of the chief ministers of Naxal-affected states held their second meeting in New Delhi on 13 April, 2006 under the chair of the prime minister. The meeting underscored the need for building up security and intelligence capabilities at state and district levels for effective anti-Naxal operations. Furthermore, the meeting stressed upon the implementation of long-term action plans for better coordination among various security outfits to ensure the protection of the railway infrastructure and the travelling public. On development front, the agenda included the following:

- need for better delivery and monitoring mechanisms in Naxal areas;
- effective implementation of land reforms,
- formulation of rehabilitation and resettlement (RR) policy for displaced tribal,
- speedy implementation of the Panchayats (Extension to Scheduled Areas) Act [PESA] 1996 etc.

Interministerial Group (IMG)

An interministerial group (IMG) was set up under the chair of additional secretary to review and address the socio-economic aspects of the Naxal problem. The IMG comprises joint secretary level officers of the main development ministries/departments of the Government of India. The IMG team will play an advisory role in the implementation of developmental schemes in the Naxal-affected areas.

Chief Ministers Meeting on Internal Security

The prime minister called a meeting of the chief ministers to discuss internal security on 5 September, 2006 and after detailed deliberations, they arrived at the following decisions:

- That terrorism and Naxalism required a firm handling. Close cooperation among the states and between the Centre and states is essential to deal with the complex internal security problems and threats.
- States agreed to take time-bound steps to improve the quality of the state special branches with focus on tactical and local intelligence generation.
- To set up an empowered group of ministers, chaired by the Union home minister, comprising select Union ministers and chief ministers to monitor the spread of Naxalism and evolve effective strategies to defuse the problem.

In pursuance of the aforementioned meeting called by the prime minister, an empowered group of ministers came into existence at the behest of the prime minister to take care of Naxal-affected states.

The Central Government views the Naxalite menace as an area of serious concern. The government remains firmly committed and determined to address the problem. Essentially, the state governments would need to pursue effective measures to improve ground level policing and development response, besides countering the negative propaganda unleashed by Naxalite.

A New Approach

The report[2] 'Development Challenges in extremist-affected Areas', looks at the Naxalite/Maoist movement in a way that is different from the prevalent official attitude and draws attention to many of the positive effects of the movement. The report rejects the official "Security Centric" approach in dealing with the movement and instead suggests an ameliorative approach with emphasis on a negotiated solution.

The expert group headed by D. Bandyopadhyay of 'Operation Barga' fame in West Bengal, lays stress on the "structural violence which is implicit in the social and economic system and which in the opinion of its authors prompts the radical groups to justify their own violent acts.

From the investigation carried out by the Planning Commission group of experts in the Naxalite areas, it appears that the Maoists are actually carrying out the reforms that the executive ought to have implemented, and are replacing the judiciary and the police by ensuring law and order for the poor and the oppressed. Commenting on the "People's Courts" set up by the Naxalite in these areas of control, the report observes that disputes are resolved in a rough and ready manner, and generally in the interest of the weaker party.

Their findings also reveal how despite change of government, successive rulers who are elected use and misuse laws to suppress the poor and the disadvantaged. There is a design behind this continuity. The rulers irrespective of party affiliations are lackadaisical and sloppy in implementing pro-poor legal measures. For instance, the Government of Andhra Pradesh sat with the then People's War Group [now merged into Communist Party of India, Maoist] in October, 2004, and agreed to a ceasefire till 16 December that year, and promised to consider in the meantime the Naxalite's main demand for distribution of land among the landless. However, when the then Congress Government failed to keep that promise, the Naxalite stepped in to distribute the land. The government retaliated immediately by sending its police which gunned down Naxalite cadres in the forests of Warangal, West Godavari and other districts in January 2005, writes Sumanta Banerjee in[3] EPW of May [24-30], 2008.

The demand for redistribution of land is the basic demand, which the landless people have right to raise as the land originally belonged to the community [Henry Maine] and it was only through operation of unjust system, some people happen to own more lands than others. Secondly, this is the undisputed and well-declared policy of Central and state governments through all the successive ten Five Year Plans. Thirdly, this is the simplest administrative manoeuvre because surplus lands have already come into the custody of the state governments by operation of Ceiling laws, which have constitutional protection under IX Schedule of the Constitution of India and are not justiciable. Fourthly, they have identified the people below poverty line [BPL] in every village.

If popular governments avoid this simple administrative work just because the stakes of a handful of people will be hurt, they have no legitimate right to be in power. They have to care for dumb majority of the country who have taken to arms against their double standard and the rest are in the process of taking up arms against the so-called democratic governments. Land is the dearest asset to the villagers because they do not part with land unlike other assets. Therefore, even in this era of economic liberalization, the land is the most important ambition of the villagers. Popular governments should pool their resources to purchase the land and distribute the same among the landless or poor villagers. They should do this on the model of "Homestead and Kitchen Garden Scheme" in West Bengal. If the persons at the helm of affairs take the required measures, the existing availability of land in government land bank will suffice for next ten years. Nevertheless, this is possible if the administration distributes surplus land among the landless with a missionary zeal. However, if they do it as a routine it is nothing but mutations and conversions of land and making land titles available for the needs of industries and commerce. The revenue machinery has to rise to recognize their age-old friends in villages and care for them because they land have-nots are presently at the worst crossroad of the history.

Along with distribution of surplus land, the authorities should guide and help them to undertake the improvement of lands given under the Bhoodan or wasteland on the pattern of Prime Minister Rozgar Yojna or PM Sarak Yojna. This will check the migration of the poor villagers to the urban areas. After distribution of land among the landless is complete, next step is to identify the sharecroppers. They have no right to the ownership of the land they cultivate.

The government has set up a high-powered National Land Reforms Council [NLRC][4] under the prime minister to make recommendations for completion of unfinished agenda on land reforms in the country. In addition to NLRC, the government has set up another committee under the minister for rural development. The task of this committee would be to monitor the implementation of the recommendations made by NLRC.

I conclude my article with a conviction that what is required is the political will and the ability to extract work from the crafty senior to junior-most babus, bureaucrats because only then the landless will get their share of land. In this way, the government will achieve two successes: One, fulfilment of its promise to allot land to the landless; two, this success will mark the end of Naxalism.

Conclusion

To tackle Naxalism, police and paramilitary forces engaged in the anti-Naxalite operation have to equip themselves with sophisticated weapons. They have to gear up intelligence network. They have to isolate them from common people. They have to draw proper strategy like army before undertaking any operation. The local police who have become demoralized on the ground, have to be geared up. Their morale has to be strengthened. The officers will have to lead first. Training in jungle and guerilla warfare will have to be imparted to them and separate units will have to be created with young energetic and courageous personnel. Ultimately nothing succeeds like success.

Endnotes

1. The Telegraph : Calcutta, 23 May, 2008 under title 'Red run 7 to 16 States in two years'.
2. The Financial Express : New Delhi, 29 October, 2007 under the heading "Manmohan to head Land Reforms Council".
3. Banerjee, Sumanta : On the Naxalite Movement : A Report with difference' EPW, Vol XLIII No. 21, May 24-30, 2008.
4. Annual Report : Government of India, Ministry of Home Affairs 2007-08 Department of Internal Security

6

Riot Control

Inadequacies of the Current Equipments and the Quest for Effective Technologies

Dr NC Asthana, IPS*

THE BASIC implement of the police is the baton/ stick/lathi[1]. In India, bamboo sticks of various lengths were used earlier. Most of the police forces have now dispensed with the bamboo stick under an argument that the bamboo stick being heavy and inflexible could break bones and if struck on the

* The writer was IG in CRPF

head, could inflict fatal injuries. They have been replaced by cane sticks or polycarbonate pipes of lengths varying from 32 inches to 39 inches which being flexible, can cause only superficial injuries. Western police forces use either a solid wood baton or telescoping steel batons up to 26 inches long.

The polycarbonate pipe or cane is of any use only against absolutely unarmed opponents who are incapable of offering any resistance. Contrary to the pseudo human rights activists' argument, it is particularly useless in India where the agitators are frequently armed with solid bamboo sticks, hockey sticks, cricket/baseball bats, swords, other sharp-edged weapons, chains, iron rods, and even guns. Such mobs are generally not encountered in the West and hence they are incapable of understanding the problem.

The basic drawback of a lathi, short baton or the telescoping steel rod is that for them to be used against even unarmed opponents, the policemen have to close in. Unless the policemen happen to be present in insufficient strength, they run the risk of getting isolated and lynched by the mob. This has happened frequently in India, recent example being the first Gujjar[2] agitation in Rajasthan where several policemen were killed. It is suicidal to tackle opponents armed with weapons mentioned above because they are all capable of inflicting fatal wounds.

And when you have mobs that are pelting stones by bare hands or slings using centrifugal force (called gophan, gophiya, gophni, gophna, or gumphani in Hindustani) there is no way the police can even close in under the barrage of high velocity stones weighing anywhere from 100 g to 500 g which are capable of knocking out a man with riot helmet on his head and inflicting a fatal wound if he happens to be inadequately protected.

Polycarbonate riot shields weighing up to even 4.5 kg each are known to have broken under the impact of such stones. The 2.5 kg variety breaks all too often. Stones weighing 8-10 kg are hurled from close quarters on vehicles frequently break bulletproof glass also even if they are protected further by stout wire meshes outside. Photographic evidence of all the above is available. Slings throw stones on a flatter trajectory and reduce reaction time if thrown from rooftops, they are indefensible.

Telescope baton

Tear Gas Grenades and Shells: Tear gas grenades have a fundamental problem of low range. Policemen who have to lob tear gas grenades must necessarily be within the range of those people who could be throwing stones at them. This makes the policemen vulnerable. That leaves the tear gas shell as the only viable option. At times, a direct hit from the shell on a sensitive spot could be fatal for susceptible individuals. This complicates the situation in a pseudo humanistic society.

Tear gas is not at all effective in open spaces. If there is a wind blowing, it reduces the effect of the gas. In most places people have learnt to adopt some improvised protective measures like using a mask of wet cloth over the face. The cleverer people wet it with apple-cider vinegar or lemon juice for added protection. A large number of recorded footage is available to prove that people who are used to agitations and have faced tear gas earlier do not bother about it. Only those who face it for the first time are likely to be dispersed by it. More commonly, the rioters pick up all but the disintegrating type shells and throw them back on the police.

Stun Grenades: Stun grenades were never designed to be used on a mob in an open space. If used in the open, it may disorientate a man who is within a couple of yards of the device but not beyond.

Stinger and Marker Grenades: The stinger grenade does not hurt more than a rubber bullet or plastic pellet. As far a marker grenade is concerned, it is of more use in collecting evidence than in dispersing a crowd.

Rubber Bullets/Plastic Pellets/Bean Bag Rounds: Once hailed as the panacea for riot control, all of these have proved to be ineffective in the long run for the simple reason that the rioters do know that, in the normal course of events they are not going to kill them. Once they see the special gun that fires them, they recognize it. Then all they have to do is to get psychologically prepared for that little pain when the round hits them. Freak fatalities are known to have resulted at times with rubber bullets/plastic pellets.

Water Cannon: Water cannons have the following intrinsic limitations:

- The carrier is big and unmanoeuvrable. Hence, it cannot be taken into narrow lanes or even over broken ground. The range is just about 50-60 yards.
- If you increase elevation for range, the jet disperses in flight and loses sting.
- The jet is so visible and its trajectory so obvious that it is extremely easy to dodge it.
- It does not really hurt badly even if you take it on the chest.

Compressed Air Weapons : Compressed air weapons like the FN303 were designed to fire projectiles containing a non-toxic granulated bismuth forward payload which breaks upon the impact thereby reducing the chances of penetration. As such it has even less of a deterrent effect.

Electric Shock Weapons Like Taser: Delivering a very high voltage shock at a very low amperage current, they are extremely effective against violent individuals, but there is no way one could imagine using them against a mob while one man goes down, others could tear the policeman apart.

The Psychology of a Riotous Mob

Violent mobs in countries like India have had a long history of lynching policemen whenever they get a chance, whatever be their purpose—most readers would be able to recall the Chauri Chaura police station incident during the freedom movement. The reasons are partly historical. The rulers of India, local or central have traditionally given such bad governance and the employees of the rulers have had such a terrible record of ill-treating the people that the public, in its collective subconscious, harbours deep hatred towards the employees of the State. The violence against the policemen is just one manifestation of this pent-up hatred of centuries. The other reasons include an utter disregard for law and the authority of law. Such people believe that the system would never be able to deliver justice, a belief which is partly justified by poor governance and a system that favours the rich and the influential and hence their belief that there is nothing wrong if they take the law into their own hands.

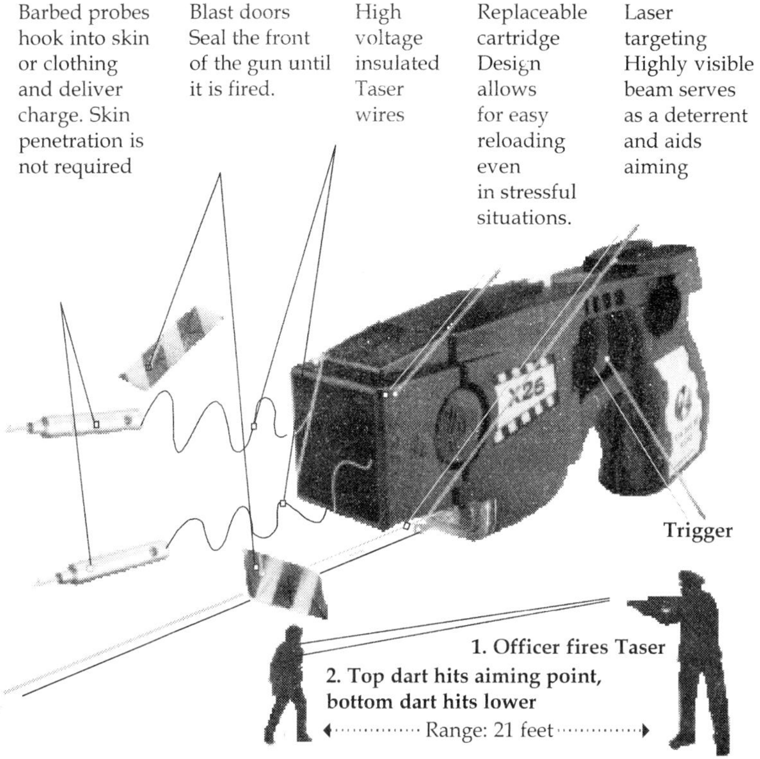

Working of a Taser X26

Photo Source: Taser International, Mc Clatchy Tribune

Mob violence could be incited by a variety of reasons having little common in them at a psychological level; however, there is a common thread; violent mobs are known to abandon reason completely and the monster that lurks underneath is unleashed a belief bolstered by the anonymity offered by the mob and a track record that mob violence has hardly ever got punished by law.

The police, being the most visible instrument of the State and also its coercive arm, invites a greater virulence from the mobs. Such mobs are not deterred by the traditional less-than-lethal devices. The reason is that they understand only the language of violence. They are deterred only when they see blood; yet the dilemma of the State is that it cannot afford to shed the blood of its people wantonly.

A Unique and most effective Weapon for Riot Control

The professional issue therefore before us is to find a method of dealing with violent mobs that will have an immediate impact upon the subliminal instincts of the mob and yet it would not be lethal.

Our contention is that if there is any weapon which does not draw blood, it would not deter a riotous mob. Hence the weapon of choice must be one which draws blood. We also contend that the weapon must belong to a category with which people are intimately familiar. Now a weapon which is absolutely unfamiliar may provoke extreme reactions. People may either dismiss it as a useless weapon and ignore it or develop extreme fright. In a real riotous situation where lives could be lost the police cannot afford to take chances. Firearms are weapons with which mankind is familiar since centuries and knows their effect too.

This means that we recommend firearms. Ignorant people could jump and claim that we are recommending lethal weapons. It is not so.

We, from our independent and the first-of-its-kind research in the whole world, have determined firearm projectiles that would draw blood and even injure a man but not kill him. We arrived at this conclusion after a great deal of experimental research to determine blood loss and consequent effects of gunshots on live animals. To our knowledge no experiments have been conducted anywhere in the world to determine the effect of gunshot wounds on live animals. In the USA, some experiments were conducted on cadavers. However, cadaver experiments can give a reasonable idea of only the penetration of the projectile and not blood loss. Thus a critical parameter remains undetermined. We have conducted the experiment on live animals and that too without violating any ethical considerations.

The animal selected for this purpose was an antelope called Nilgai (Boselaphus tragocamelu). The hunting of this animal is permitted by law in the State of Uttar Pradesh, during certain seasons when they start destroying crops. Nilgai stand 4-5 foot at the shoulder and are 6-6.6 foot long. Mature Nilgai typically weigh 120-240 kg. By size and weight this is the only destroyable animal experiments on which can correspond to the adult human body. The skin and musculature of this animal offers resistance to a projectile similar to that from the human body. Since the animal is larger in size than humans, proportionate blood loss in humans of 70 kg was calculated.

Several captured animals of this type were shot at from a distance of 50 yards in the trunk with different shot loads and different chokes (ranging from cylinder, skeet, improved cylinder, modified, and improved modified to full choke) and the penetration and blood loss determined. No animal was critically injured and all of them were released after treatment. We experimented with various shots ranging from shot sizes 1 (shot size 0.143 inch/100 pellets to an ounce),

B (0.154/80), BB (0.161/70), BBB (0.170/60), A (0.180/50), AA (0.194/40), AAA (0.203/35), SSSSSG (0.214/30), SSSSG (0.227/25), and SSSG (0.245/20) to SSG (0.269/15).

The weapon finally selected is the 12 bore pump action shotgun with standard American full choke or its equivalent (pattern percentage 75%) firing a one ounce load with Eley 'standard' cartridge (such as the Grand Prix) with an 'observed' velocity of 1070 feet per second and 'striking' velocity of 696 feet per second at 50 yards. The projectile is English size AAA lead shot containing pellets of diameter 0.203 inch (5.16 mm) with each pellet weighing 12.50 grains (0.81 g) and 35 pellets to an ounce (12.3 per 10 g). Equivalent shot sizes according to different countries' specifications can be easily calculated.

We found that shot sizes smaller than AAA do not cause much blood loss in a 70 kg man that would worry him, whereas shot sizes bigger than AAA cause blood loss which may be unacceptably higher. Of course, bigger shots may be used at longer ranges or with reduced choke to yield the same effect. It may be kept in mind that the SSG is the typical combat load which will result in a sure kill on humans.

The AAA shot does not result in a wound which causes internal injuries. Even on abdomen the penetration is not beyond the muscle wall. It is therefore found to be the ideal riot control shot which will draw blood, may cause a man to faint and even incapacitate him out of sheer fright of having been shot, but would not kill him.

Since the police would be using firearms, the rioters would be convinced that lethal fire may result and hence there would be deterrent effect. Yet it is only the police who would know that the shot selected is not lethal. For emergencies, the policemen may keep SSG load or even rifled slugs to defend themselves.

Emerging Technologies

Several new technologies are being tried for riot control. The most promising of them is the so-called 'Active Denial System' a vehicle mounted system which radiates a beam of microwaves of 95 GHz frequency. The penetration of the microwaves is only about 1/64th of an inch in the skin and they produce a burning sensation. While not actually burning the skin, the burning sensation is similar to that of a light bulb being pressed against the skin. The focused beam can be directed at targets at a range of about half a kilometer, or about 550 yards. The American defense contractor, Raytheon, has developed a smaller version of the ADS, named the Silent Guardian. The problem with the ADS is that there is very little research on it that has been published in peer-reviewed journals.

Some sonic weapons are currently in limited use or in research and development; others exist only in the realm of science fiction. Extremely high-power sound waves can break the eardrums of a target and cause severe pain or disorientation. Less powerful sound waves can cause humans to experience nausea or discomfort. Researchers also found that low frequency sonar exposure could result in significant cavitations, hypothermia, and tissue shearing. Sufficient research on the subject is yet to be done to prove its efficacy in riot-control.

Endnotes

1. Lathi a heavy pole or stick, especially one used as a club by police.
2. An ethnic group in Rajasthan, India

7

Police Firearms and Weapons

Dr NC Asthana, IPS*

THE FUNDAMENTAL PROBLEM with the weaponry for the police in India has been that the police system, in its legendary intellectual bankruptcy, has had never applied mind to demand and develop weapons suited specifically for the police. In terms of its equipment, the police in India have subconsciously adapted themselves as a service secondary to the army to such an extent that even for controlling riots, something which is exclusively their domain, they are not ashamed when the governments call in the army for a job which is not theirs by training or temperament. It is not surprising that the police weaponry has followed the army without even realizing that they are using weapons designed for a military context and not specifically for the police. As

* The writer is presently posted with CRPF

a result, the Indian police is perhaps the only police force in the world that has used and has been using military firearms for over a century a great testimonial to its dumbness.

Way back towards the last quarter of the 19th century when the British army in India was using the Henry Martinis and the Snyder rifles, the police used flintlock muskets. When the army switched over to the Lee Enfield .303, the police took over the Henry Martinis and the Snyders. Some of these were converted into .410 smoothbore muskets, also for police use. Then the army adopted the 7.62 FN FAL and later the police too used them for quite some time, many are still in existence alongside the .303. With the advent of terrorism in the country, the police and the army came to use the same AK-47s and INSAS.

The point which the police missed all along is that a police weapon must not be designed to kill at the first instance simply because the victim could be needed further for questioning and eventual prosecution for justice. A military has no such requirement. The police weapons for regular use should have sufficient stopping power to incapacitate but not inflict a lethal wound as far as possible. For anti-terrorist operations, of course, they have to have military weapons.

The Ideal Police Handgun

The Semi-Automatic Pistol versus the Revolver Debate

Technically, the argument of the revolver being a more reliable weapon than a semi-automatic pistol has little relevance now as ammunition of a much better quality is available which seldom misfires. A pistol has the advantage of a higher magazine capacity, faster reloading, a more ergonomic grip and more safety features. Revolvers are best as backup weapons.

Is There a 'Universally' Greatest Pistol?

The fact is that there is no single pistol that can meet all the requirements of a user and thus you cannot select a 'universally' greatest pistol. Thus you can only select the best pistol for a specific purpose in mind. For example, if you have to select a pistol for VIP security then the most important feature to be kept in mind is the pointing quality of the gun, and double-action lock, that is, the absence of a safety catch and an extremely low failure rate. If you have to issue pistols to commandos or troops who may have to fight in the field then the most important consideration is the ability of the gun to function reliably even with dirt in its mechanism and a large magazine capacity.

The Browning BDA9, BDAO and BDM

The Browning, nicknamed the 'King of Nines', is a short-recoil action operated pistol against which other 9 mm pistols are measured. The Browning HP of 1935 had a single action trigger. The Browning DA (Double Action), introduced in 1983, has an increased magazine capacity of 14 rounds and an ambidextrous frame-mounted de-cocker lever. The BDA9 is a 1990 version of the DA. The BDAO is a further development with a 'double-action only' trigger, keeping the modern trend in mind.

The Walther PP and PPK

Ideal as a backup gun and also as an undercover weapon, the Walther PP and the PPK were the first double-action guns in the world with a simple reliable blowback action. The Walther PPK is a shortened version of the PP (Polizei PistolePolice Pistol; the K in PPK stands either for Kurz meaning short or Kriminal meaning the PP for the criminal police or undercover detectives. The PP comes in the 9x17 mm (9 mm Kurz or Short) caliber also but the 7.65 mm version is more famous.

The Sig-Sauer P226

This is an excellent recoil-operated double-action pistol, especially suited for VIP security in view of its pointing qualities. When the US Army conducted the so-called Great American Pistol Test (or the XM9 pistol trial) in 1984 to consider a replacement for the Colt M1911A1, the P226 and Beretta 92SB-F were the only pistols that could pass the test consisting of 85 requirements out of the mandatory 72 requirements.

The Beretta 92 SB-F

Though an excellent gun with its famous cut-away slide, the problem with the Beretta is that it is a big gun suitable only for people with large hands. It also demands good maintenance.

The Glock Family of Pistols

If you are looking for a gun that is really a product of modern high technology, it is from the Glock family of guns. The guns even look modern with their rectangular slides, unique grip and trigger guard designed for double-handed shooting. The Glock has many unconventional features. The first is its exceptionally low weight and small size. The Glock 19C is the lightest 9 mm pistol in the world. The second is the use of a special polymer for the frame and steel slide.

Ideal Police Weapons for Anti-terrorist Operations

Size and weight are important criteria. When troops have to operate in built-up areas and manoeuvre themselves into tight spaces, or scale walls etc with the rifle, the rifle must not be big or heavy. This means that the stock has to be collapsible.

In anti-terrorist operations or counter-insurgency operations (CI Ops), in stark contrast to infantry warfare, we cannot dispense with the requirement of fully automatic fire in critical situations like entering a building or a room. A sub-machine gun cannot be used effectively when you have to fire at a range of 100-200 mts say for example, when returning fire in an ambush.

The AK-47 Versus the INSre

The rifle chosen should be capable of delivering fully automatic fire. A three-round burst capability might have relevance for an infantry soldier in regular infantry warfare but it has little significance in CI Ops. In CI Ops, we certainly do not require a full length cartridge. The cartridge has to be intermediate. All these considerations leave the AK the undisputed king of the field. The INSAS comes nowhere near it. The higher muzzle velocity of the 5.56 mm bullet offers no additional advantage in CI Ops where bullets are fired at a rather low range of 100 m or so. Further, it is a scientifically established fact that the higher calibre leads to more blood loss, leading to faster incapacitation.

Sub-machine Guns (SMGs)

If you are in a situation in urban combat or even in a jungle where you want to deliver a high volume of fire in a short time but the range is not high, the accuracy is not important and you are not concerned about the penetrating power of the bullets, then the sub-machine gun is the weapon for you.

In other words, the sub-machine gun is the weapon of choice when you simply want to pump in as much lead as possible on targets which are neither far from you nor hardened. Using sub-machine guns for VIP security as you see them totted by the commandos is another example of intellectual bankruptcy of the police. The VIPs are generally to be found and likely to be attacked only in a chrowd you cannot afford to pour in a high volume of fire there indiscriminately in fact, you need a weapon like the SIG-Sauer P226 which can deliver accurate fire.

The Heckler & Koch MP-5 series and MP-5K

Adopted in 1966, the SMGs of Heckler & Koch MP-5 series are still the guns against which other SMGs are measured in terms of technical perfection. Functionally, it could be argued to be a scaled-down version of the G3 rifle, that is, a roller delayed blowback gun firing from a closed bolt. The HK MP-5K is a special compact version of the MP-5.

Combat Shotguns

The invention of the repeating shotgun made it into a weapon for the forces from a sporting weapon. For the simple reason that you throw a bunch of pellets and not just a single bullet, you can use the shotgun wherever the target is not clearly visible, some pellets would definitely get to the target!

Shotguns are therefore particularly suited for combat in urban areas, trenches or in bushes. Their basic problem is that the range is very limited; however, the shotgun has tremendous firepower within the limited range. A properly selected combat load has more man-stopping capability than any other type of ammunition. Shotguns are versatile in the sense that loads come in a wide variety and you can select your load according to your needs, can carry different types with you, and even keep a mix of several types of loads in the same magazine. The most popular combat load is the SSG (loosely called buckshot by some), which contains 9 pellets for the 12 gauge shell. You can even fire special purpose ammunition like the door buster slug or flechettes!

Basic Configurations

Basic configurations of combat shotguns are the older 'pump action' and the semi-automatic. Pump action shotguns have a serious limitation in that the reloading is quite slow. It also engages both your hands, a great handicap indeed! Hence, these shotguns are weapons of choice for short engagements or in riot control where too many rounds are not expected to be fired. Semi-automatic shotguns offer higher firepower, but their high-cost factor inhibits their use.

The Remington 870

The Remington 870 is the most popular weapon both amongst civilians and soldiers. It came into the market in 1950, and has sold well over seven million pieces. The gun comes in barrels as short as 10 inches to 18 inches and with or without pistol grips.

The Mossberg 590

The Mossberg 590 is known for its ruggedness and relatively low cost. They say that only their gun passed the US Army Mil-Spec 3443E test of the firing of 3000 shells of full-power 12 gauge SSG shot.

The Benelli M1014

The US armed forces have taken this semi-auto as a joint service combat shotgun and named it the M1014. Its functions in entirely a new method called the "auto regulating gas operated" (ARGO) system.

The Winchester 1300

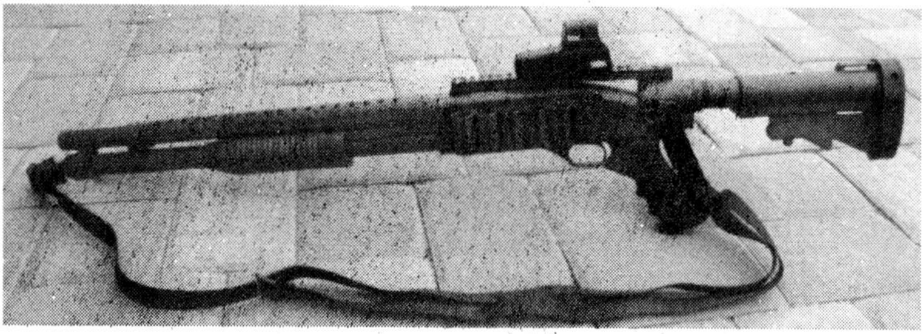

Winchester claims that theirs is one of the fastest operable pump action shotguns. Owing to the 'Speed Pump' design incorporating an innovative inertia-assisted pumping of its rotary bolt action, the Model 1300 is capable of shooting three shots in just over half a second (.56 seconds).

8

Protecting Indian Cyber Space

—Muktesh Chander, IPS*

INCREASING USE OF COMPUTERS, computer networks and communication technology has resulted in the exchange of huge amount of vital information stored and processed on computers. This is not only true for individuals, various organisations and companies but for governments and their institutions as well. The confidentiality, availability and security of this information are crucial for most organisations to run their e-commerce or e-governance model. Cyber security breaches are resulting in huge losses globally. Peculiar nature and global reach of cyber crimes have forced the organisations to take steps towards managing information security issues in a planned manner with a holistic approach. The computer professionals have realized that cyber

* The writer is presently posted at Daman & Diu Islands

security is a complex and multidisciplinary subject and simple, technological product driven, off the shelf solutions are of limited use.

Digital Society

India has embraced Integrated Computer Technology (ICT) in a big way. Private companies, government institutions, organizations and citizens are using computers and computer networks like never before. We are fast moving towards a digital society and hence we need to secure our cyber space. Cyber security is now becoming a vital subset of national security and guarding critical information and infrastructures are of paramount importance to a nation like India, which is fighting various forms of terrorism in the last several decades. Several advanced nations have realized the dangers to their cyber space and have taken steps to protect it. India needs to evolve its own strategy to protect her cyber space.

ICT Revolution and Indian Cyber Space

For the past two decades, India is witnessing a great digital revolution, which has changed our society in an unprecedented way affecting every one's life. Enabled by technology mission, abundant software talent and global effect, India is now harnessing the benefits of ICT in a big way. The talent that made India the centre of global delivery in IT over the last 15 years has now developed the skills and experience it needs to apply these knowledge at home (Nilekani, 2008). They have created internet backbones and countrywide fibre optic networks, which have brought broadband within reach of an average Indian. The

Department of telecommunication has set a target of 20 million broadband subscribers by the year 2010. Personal computer (PC) literacy in India has shown a steady growth since 2004. By September 2007, there were 46 million internet users in India showing an increase of 40 per cent over previous year. There were 23.39 lakh broadband subscribers in India as on 31 March 2007 (TRAI, 2007).

Growth in Mobile Services

Mobile subscriber base in India is also increasing very fast. In November 2008, there were 249 million users in India, an addition of about 7.6 million every month (COAI, 2008). The figure is likely to cross 560 million by 2012. Call rates, SMS and MMS services offered by mobile phone companies are becoming cheap and therefore popular among the younger generation. Value-added services like payment of bills, mobile banking, ticket reservation etc. have further added to its popularity. Mobile commerce, advanced e-mail, mobile advertising, social networking, internet surfing, and mobile gaming are likely to emerge as big markets. They expect market size of such value-added services in India to rise to Rs 22,400 crore by 2011. The cellular companies are now heading towards rural areas with value-added services, specially designed for rural population. According to internetworldstas.com, India is third among 10 top internet countries with 60 million users figuring only below China and Japan. With the trends of increased Internet usage, they forecast a growth of 32 per cent in internet advertising over the next five years to reach an estimated Rs 11 billions in 2021 (PriceWaterHouseCoopers, 2007). Indian netizens have emerged as third biggest online shoppers in the world-using credit card (Nielson, 2008).

E-commerce

Indian Railways Passenger Reservation System now caters to 5.5 lakh passenger reservations from more than 4000 terminals across the country. Even though it started late in India, now more than 80 per cent of airline tickets are sold electronically. The e-retailing has emerged as a big market where the sellers are selling almost everything from toys, books, home appliances, consumer electronic items, automobiles etc. Service sector is also following similar trends. Online jobs, matrimonial services and other classified markets have mushroomed. Digital download of music and video is poised to increase its share in e-commerce market in India. With increase in GPRS, enabled services and arrival of 3G services, mobile commerce and mobile value-added service industry (MVAS) in India will see huge growth in coming years.

India is a favoured destination for software development and outsourcing backend operations of multinational corporations all over the world. The Government policies have also been a boosting factor for BPO and software industry. Number of persons employed in the BPO sector in India has more than doubled from 220,000 in 2003-04 to 410,000 in 2005-06 with revenue growth from US $ 3.1 billions to US $ 6.3 billions (MIT, 2008). Revenue from BPO industry is likely to touch US $ 50 billions by 2012 (NASSCOM, 2008).

E-governance

The Government of India has launched a National e-governance plan (NeGP) in 2006 comprising 27 Mission Mode Projects with 10 components with a vision to make government services accessible to citizens in their locality through common service centres (CSC). The objectives are to ensure accessibility, transparency, efficiency and reliability in governance. The NeGP envisages establishment of 100,000 CSCs in 600,000 villages of India, which will act as the nodal centres for e-governance delivery points in the locality of citizens. They have earmarked Rs 5742 crore for the scheme. National portal of India now offers as many as 155 online services in 14 sectors and the list is increasing fast. (National portal, 2008). It is obvious that the Indian Cyber Space is growing exponentially and so is our digital dependence on it.

Cyber Crimes in India

Like other developed and developing countries, India is also facing cyber crime challenges. Before the enactment of IT Act, the police registered the cyber crimes under various sections of Indian Penal Code. Since 2000, the police register the cyber crimes under IPC as well as IT Act.

Some of the cities where software industries are situated are showing sharp increase in cyber crime cases registered under IT Act, 2000 as seen in Table 1.

Table 1: Cyber Crime Statistics of some of the Cities in India

City	2003	2004	2005	2006	2007	2008
Delhi	4	4	10	5	10	33
Bangalore*	7	14	38	27	40	126
Gurgaon	1	–	4	2	5	12
Chennai	6	10	20	7	4	47
Pune	4	6	9	10	14	43
Hyderabad	3	–	–	–	2	5
Sub Total	**25**	**34**	**77**	**49**	**70**	**255**
Total India	**60**	**68**	**179**	**142**	**217**	**666**

*Bangalore Cyber Crime Police Station for Karnataka.

The police registered 217 cyber crime cases under IT Act during the year 2007 as compared to 142 cases during the previous year thereby reporting an increase of 52.8 per cent. Giving the break-up the police revealed that 45 per cent of the cases related to cyber pornography, 35 per cent to hacking. (NCRB, 2007). Cyber crime is cognizable in smaller towns in India. Worldwide trends of cyber crime are alarming and in India we need to gear up for the challenges ahead (Muktesh 1, 2009).

Vulnerability of Indian Cyber Space

Preparedness for cyber security of Indian organizations, both in public and private sectors, is far from satisfactory and some of the recent happenings are a pointer to the level of existing vulnerability and gaping holes in the Indian cyber security environment. Nearly one in three Indian organizations suffered some financial loss because of cyber attack (CIO, 2006). In 2007, a Swedish "ethical hacker" blogged details of e-mail accounts and passwords of several Indian government institutions, including Defence Research and Development Organization, National Defence Academy and Indian embassies in several countries (DNA, 2007). In December 2009, all digital records of details pertaining to gate passes allotted to vehicles for the year 2007, which enabled them to enter UP assembly building, were lost following a virus infection in the computer. The loss assumes significance in view of the attack on Parliament in 2001 and recent terror attack in Mumbai (*The Hindu,* 2008). In October 2008, Noida Police arrested five educated cyber criminals after they illegally transferred Rs 1.66 crores from the bank account of a victim by hacking into his internet bank account (*Hindustan Times,* 2008). A major Manesar based multinational IT company has reportedly decided to shift its $ 10 million R & D facility to Australia due to a recent incident of IPR data theft in electronic form which caused it an estimated loss of Rs. 754 crores (*Expressindia,* 2006). Kingfisher airline reportedly incurred a loss of Rs 17 crores and several other airline companies suffered similar losses due to fraudulent ticket purchases from their online booking systems. According to a survey conducted by Read minds, 30 per cent of banks are reported to have become victims of identity theft/phishing during last one year. Besides, more than 57 per cent of banks still do not have a dedicated budget for online security (Read minds, 2008). During 2008; the hackers defaced five thousand four hundred and seventy-five Indian websites. In the year 2007, Computer Emergency Response Team of India (CERT-IN) received three hundred and ninety-two phishing complaints involving banks and financial institutions. Security incidents handled by (CERT-IN) in 2007 have gone up by 124 per cent over the previous year. It tracked 146891 bot-equipped computers in the country (CERT-IN, 2008). The Indian Mujahideen sent terror e-mails through unsecured Wi-Fi networks. This happened after the recent serial blasts in Delhi, Ahmedabad, and Jaipur. These highlight the cyber security breaches, which may be the tip of the iceberg. General awareness about cyber security amongst average Indian computer users is alarmingly low and so are the investigating capabilities of cyber security breaches by police in most of the states except in metropolitan cities.

Critical Information Infrastructure

Critical Information Infrastructure (CII) is a subset of all vital installations. As more and more critical systems in vital sectors in India are getting computerized and linked to networks, their vulnerability is increasing. Some of them are:

- Telecommunications and Internet backbones.
- Electrical power generation and distribution systems including nuclear power stations.
- Banking and financial systems including stock exchanges.
- Transportation control systems.
- Communication systems including satellite communication, cell phone communication, microwave links, GPS Navigation, Direct to Home broadcasts.
- e-governance and e-commerce
- Military and Defence installations including their C4I (Command, Control, Communication, computers and Intelligence).

- Emergency response systems like police, ambulance and Fire Brigade.

These sectors are crucial for national economy, security and governance. Besides, these sectors are interdependent in a complex way and their proper functioning is important to many other infrastructures. In general, one of the remarkable features of modern, computer-based society is that a seemingly endless series of small details must function correctly and in cooperation to maintain the numerous processes that we take for granted. A single "bug", the smallest aberration, so subtle as to be virtually invisible to the naked eye, can theoretically initiate a complex chain of events, the effects of which manifest at a national or even global level. Protecting these critical information infrastructures (CII) against disruption of any kind is increasingly crucial in maintaining both domestic stability and national security (C I I, 2006).

While we are embracing the Information Technology in a big way, we are realizing that without adequate security, all the new systems may create more problems than solve them (Sangi, 2006). It happened when submarine cable connection between India and rest of the world was disrupted. When Estonia faced coordinated cyber attacks on its critical information infrastructure for three weeks in April 2007, NATO leaders realized the need for a systematic strategy to deal with cyber attacks. In the recently notified Information Technology (Amendment) Act 2008, the Government of India has recognized the importance of (CII) and has made provision for declaring any organization as the national nodal agency in respect of critical information infrastructure protection.

Cyber War and Cyber Terrorism

"Why to send a bullet where you can send a byte" is the new phrase in cyber space. Cyber weapons can create more havoc in a short time and on a wider target area than the conventional weapons. If used intelligently, on selected target systems in unison, these cyber weapons act as, "Digital Intercontinental Ballistic Missiles" (Muktesh 2, 2003). For modern war C4I (command, control, communication, computers and intelligence) are the critical factors. Dayal (2005) suggested that tools of cyber terrorism are exceptional force multipliers when such tools are integrated with conventional weapons causing large-scale havoc and disruption.

Several nations have taken a serious note of the cyber skirmishes between group of hackers of various countries such as Hezbollah and Hamas, Palestine and Israel, America and China, Russia and Georgia, India and Pakistan. Cyber Terrorism threats are a matter of concern, several nations have started gearing themselves for such an eventuality in near future, and many have conducted mock exercises. Realising this danger Indian legislature has defined and prescribed punishment for "Cyber Terrorism" in IT (Amendment) Act 2008 but we have to go a long way in this direction.

Cyber Security

Cyber security is a broad subject and various definitions are available. American National Standard

Institute (ANSI, 2008) defines cyber security as the protection of any computer system, software program and data against unauthorized disclosure, transfer, modification or destruction, whether accidental or intentional. Information Technology (Amendment) Act 2008 has defined cyber security as protecting information, equipment, devices, computer, computer resources, communication device and information stored therein from unauthorized access, use disclosure, disruption, modification or destruction. It is not possible to ensure cyber security by some software. Those responsible for security have to take care of it as a whole.

CIA TRIAD

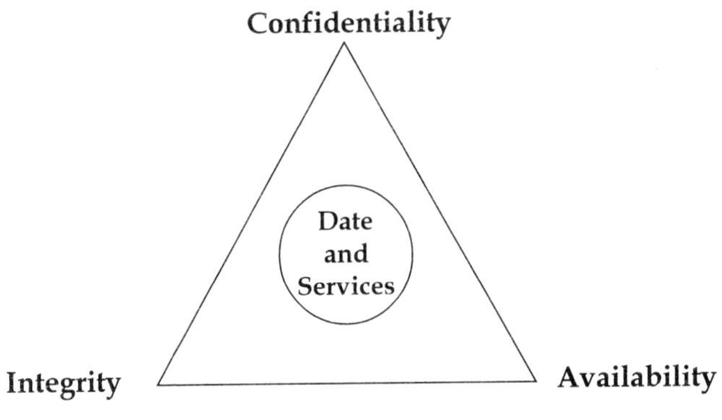

Cyber Security stands on a tripod of confidentiality, integrity and availability of data and services commonly known as CIA triad as shown in Picture 1.

- Confidentiality means ensuring that the information does not fall in the hands of unauthorized persons and is accessible only to authorized persons. It must also remain confidential while in transit.

- Integrity means that the information remain untempered while in transit or in storage. Integrity is often discussed as having two dimensions of data integrity and systematically.
- Availability means the information is accessible to authorized persons whenever required without diminishing its value.

National Cyber Space Protection Strategy

Several advanced nations have included protection of their cyber space as a part of their national security. The USA had highlighted it in a document "National Strategy to Secure Cyberspace" as early as 2003. Cyber security strategy of the United Kingdom for safety, security and resilience in cyber space has been just released (UK, 2009). Learning lessons from cyber attacks in 2007, Estonian ministry of defence came up with their cyber security strategy (Estonia, 2008). India also needs to develop its own cyber security strategy keeping in view the situation in its neighbourhood.

Following steps need to be initiated immediately.

- Formulate National Cyber Security Strategy.
- Identify, categorize and prioritize national information systems and critical information infrastructures whether in private or government sector and make them resilient and secure. There isneed for mandatory certification of such infrastructure under ISO 27001:2005 in a time bound manner. We also need to develop our own information security standards and make them mandatory for critical sectors.

- Establish National Critical Information Infrastructure Protection Authority.
- Appoint an apex level agency to oversee countrywide implementation of the cyber security measures.
- Allocate sufficient resources and funds for national cyber defence.
- Strengthen legal framework with laws similar to the US laws like Federal Information Security Management Act, Health Insurance Portability and Accountability Act, Gramm-Leach-Bliley Act etc.
- Carry nationwide mock cyber security exercises out to test cyber preparedness and take corrective steps accordingly.
- Increase cyber surveillance, investigation and detection skills and capabilities of Indian intelligence and police organizations (Muktesh 3, 2003).
- Introduce cyber security courses in higher education to build a cadre of information security specialists and cyber warriors to strengthen our cyber defence mechanism.
- Strengthen interagency and interministerial coordination on cyber security issues.
- Increase information security awareness and education of computer users public and all stakeholders. There is a need to introduce nationwide culture of cyber security.
- Promote use of encryption and digital signatures by departments dealing with sensitive information.
- Promote interdisciplinary research and development in cyber security.

- Develop indigenous cyber forensics, diagnostics and security tools suitable for Indian conditions.
- Secure participation of industry, academia and NGOs for a coordinated response to cyber threats
- Collaborate with other countries/regional and international bodies for tackling cyber crime and information security issues. In this regard there is need to sign international and regional treaties.

Conclusion

As we protect our physical boundaries, in the information age we need to protect our cyber space from invisible enemies. Digital India needs a digital fortress with an aim of information assurance to all its netizens. Lessons learnt from cyber attacks on other nations and their cyber defence strategies could be of great help in preparing our own cyber defence mechanism in the 21st century. We cannot wait for a disaster to occur before we act.

9

Deterioration of the Police System

— Thakur Shailendra Nath* —

RECENT GLOBAL RECESSION has only a mild effect on the Indian economy, and the country is basking in the euphoria about having emerged as a major power in the belief that both economic development and security are on the right track.

India can be called a soft state, because rule of law has been given a go-by in many parts of the country. The spectre that haunts most political parties is the fear of losing their vote banks. They are hesitant to voice their protest against criminals or gangs that can raise the banner of religious or regional identity. Though everybody, regardless of religion or region is equal before the law and the Indian Constitution provides that there should not be any discrimination

* The writer is an officer in Customs and Central Excise Department

against one or the other for political or any other considerations, but in real life it is not being practised. Blatant violations by the rich and influential have become commonplace. And whenever the government turns a blind eye, it lays the foundation for the breakdown of the entire system of governance and theory of broken window syndrome truly applies. The faults in the system are being exploited by forces hostile to India. Too many concessions are enjoyed by all sorts of people and groups to carry on their illegal activities. In such a situation the police which is required to maintain law and order is helpless and is in a dilemma to take appropriate and stringent action against the law breakers. This attitude of the police is causing a frightening decline in the ability and willingness to do their job. The country is experiencing an unprecedented decline in the efficacy of the politico-administrative structure. Politicisation of the state institutions has seriously eroded their credibility and effectiveness. All-pervasive corruption is eating into the vitals of the Indian state. Even judiciary is not free from it.

India's internal security challenges have become progressively more complex since the late '70s. But the government is still looking for soft options and simplistic solutions by underplaying the problems or by trying to pass on the buck for the present mess to the states. It is evident that short-term electoral advantages have taken precedence over the requirements of national security.

The growing ineffectiveness of the tools of governance, especially the police and criminal justice system is one of the major causes for the growth of extremists and militant forces. The increasing politicization and breakdown of the command and control system in the police and intelligence agencies has allowed the leadership in many states to pass into the hands of officers known for their flexibility than for their merit and leadership qualities. The perception that the state is weak and unable to provide protection to life and property of its people encourages the forces of lawlessness. The dissatisfaction of the people should be addressed by taking possible steps considering social, economic and political factors. Unfortunately, instead of concentrating on strategies to address these grievances, only enquiry commissions are being repeatedly appointed without taking any concrete steps. This has resulted in further reinforcing a sense of victimization among the alienated communities. Suffering from a sense of injustice, they readily believe the false propaganda that state is discriminating against them. Therefore, the government has only made the task of police in dealing with the secessionist and

terrorist groups more difficult. Any action against the suspected persons is seen as an assault on the entire community by the large section of people in that community. With the state structure losing its credibility, legitimacy and effectiveness, the job of the police has become more difficult.

The security forces are stretched over vast areas, in large parts of India's vast rural expanse, and pitted against their own people. Large deployment of security forces suffering from a siege mentality in far-flung areas, in fact provides more targets to the extremists. An important point is that senior bureaucrats, police and intelligence officers should be made accountable for their bad advice and failures in the field. Few black sheep in the police who indulge in corruption have given a bad name to the entire force and need to be weeded out. There are still quite a few people in the police who are honest out of conviction and not fear. However, for most of them honesty begins and ends with them. It may be advisable to keep one's integrity intact but it is not enough if corruption is allowed to flourish right under their nose. They are obliged to catch and root out corruption and to protect the honest. They seem too much in love with their white clothes to take such a risk. One cannot fight corruption in white clothes, as it inevitably involves mudslinging. White clothes and fighting corruption do not go hand in hand. To challenge corruption, one has to don khakis or fatigues and take on stones and brickbats that come thick and fast. You take off your khakis only when the job is accomplished.

10

Problem Oriented Policing

PM Nair, IPS*

HUMAN TRAFFICKING is one of the gravest violations of human rights. It is not only a manifestation of deprivation of human dignity but also commercialization of human life by human predators. The numbers of people who are trafficked, especially women, children and those from the vulnerable sections of society, are indeed mindboggling. A fair assessment shows that no place is completely free from human trafficking, be it a source, transit or destination.

Need for Rehabilitation

A study (Action Research) conducted by the National Human Rights Commission (NHRC) show that one of

* The writer is presently posted with the Central Reserve Police Force (CRPF)

the major drawbacks in the response in human trafficking is that there is no institutionalized mechanism for addressing the post-rescue activities. After rescue of the trafficked person, there is no attention to the victim's rehabilitation, as several police officials think that it is not their domain; the police become busy in the investigative process. The Indian Police Act 1861 mandates police with two duties, namely, (a) Prevention of crime and (b) Investigation and detection of crime. The important aspect of "Protection" i.e., rehabilitation of the victim is a function which needs to be expressly mandated in the Act. However, even in the present context, no law enforcement agency can escape this mandate, especially because rehabilitation is the best method and an essential requirement for preventing re-trafficking. So far, there is no provision for looking after the rescued persons. More often, rescued persons are un-attended and uncared for, making them an easy target of traffickers. Therefore, re-trafficking is one of the major challenges in the existing response pattern. The NHRC study shows that almost 50 per cent of the rescued victims are re-trafficked at some point of time. Appropriate institutionalized mechanisms for providing care and for ensuring rehabilitation are therefore, essential to forestall the re-trafficking of the rescued persons. Policing has to be problem-oriented. It has to be reality-based. More often it is not so because they have neither studied, nor understood, nor analysed the problem. However, the case of human trafficking is an exception, as the NHRC has researched the problem and so the remedies and solutions borne out of the research are within the realm of knowledge.

To address these gaps thrown up by the NHRC research, and in consonance with the recommendations of the Action Research, they decided to set up "Integrated Anti-Human Trafficking Unit (AHTU)" to address human trafficking.

Origin of Anti-human Trafficking Unit

The Ministry of Home Affairs (MHA), Government of India, in partnership with United Nations Office on Drugs and Crime (UNODC), New Delhi, with support from the US government, instituted a project on "Strengthening the law enforcement response in India against trafficking in persons through training and capacity building". This project, which commenced in mid-2006, had the mandate to undertake all initiatives in human trafficking. Under the mandate, the problem-oriented policing was given due attention. Thus, they decided to set up the Integrated Anti-Human Trafficking Unit (AHTU) as one of the main activities in the project. The umbilical cord of AHTU with the Action Research meant that the AHTU represented the 'action' part of a research finding. It is indeed very rare to carry out a research on a police problem. Rarer still is the implementation of the research findings by translating them into a police function. AHTU, therefore, stands out as an exception, an embodiment of action based on research.

Anti-human Trafficking Units Created

Anti-Human Trafficking Unit is a comprehensive and cohesive body set up to address human trafficking from a holistic perspective and in an integrated manner. It is essentially a task force, constituted within the police department with the cooperation of the officials of different departments in the state, including the prosecution directorate, the department of women and child development, department of labour, health and the civil society representatives. So far, nine AHTUs have been set up under the MHA-UNODC project in four states, namely Andhra Pradesh, Bihar, Goa and West Bengal.

The Launch

22 January 2007 marked a watershed in response to human trafficking in India. A small step, yet a new beginning, turned out to be a great initiative. This was the launch of the first AHTU in India in the state of Andhra Pradesh. The home minister of Andhra Pradesh inaugurated three units at three places in Andhra Pradesh: Hyderabad, Anantapur and Eluru. The launch began with the flagging of three vehicles exclusively dedicated for anti-human trafficking work. As the second state in India to join this process, the chief minister of Goa on 24 March 2007 inaugurated the Goa unit of AHTU. The chief minister of West Bengal on 28 June 2007 launched the West Bengal unit of AHTU. The fourth state to set up the AHTU is Bihar, where the chief minister launched three anti-human trafficking units on 7 November 2007.

By involving the highest political, administrative and police functionaries of the state, the mission of anti-human trafficking has received the top priority. During the launch, the chief minister of Bihar spoke

Home Minister of Andhra Pradesh launched the first Integrated Anti-Human Trafficking Unit (AHTU) in India on 22 January 2007, along with UNODC and state government officials.

about the need for integrated action by all the responders and appreciated AHTU as a symbol of synergy and commitment.

The home minister of AP said that AHTU is the need of the day as it is an embodiment of partnership. The chief minister of Goa hailed it as a sustainable initiative. The chief minister of West Bengal acclaimed AHTU as an appropriate mechanism to provide relief and succour to the many whose voices nobody heard before.

AHTUs are much more than Vehicles

Various state governments launched the AHTU by releasing or flagging off vehicles though it was only a symbolic action. Teamwork was the main aim of this mission. It was a medium of addressing the problem, rather policing the problem. In order to facilitate proper functioning, the project also provided the following facilities to each AHTU:

- Vehicle, one per AHTU.
- Protocol for action.
- Computer systems and accessories.
- Three cell phones for each AHTU.
- Adequate handouts to meet the post-rescue operations.
- Training, capacity building and empowerment of the stakeholders in the AHTU.
- Resource materials in the form of SOPs, handbooks and list of Do's and Don'ts for various functionaries in the AHTU.
- Protocol for setting up of AHTU.

The Protocol of AHTU

Since AHTUs are innovative institutions, a protocol was prepared by UNODC with the help of concerned stakeholders. This protocol explains the role of various agencies, the mechanisms of coordination, the method of developing and sustaining synergy in the activities and ensuring accountability of the stakeholders. The bottom line of the protocol is that all activities are for the benefit of the rescued persons. The protocol is available on the website unodc.org/India. As a part of the protocol, certain agencies have entered into MoU (Memorandum of Understanding). The MoU between CID West Bengal and NGO, SANLAAP, is a case in point.

Empowerment of the Stakeholders

The empowerment of the stakeholders started with the training of those involved in the programme, including the NGOs. These were tasked with specific activities, based on the core competence. The empowerment process was extensive enough to cover police officers, prosecutors, forensic personnel, health providers, counsellors etc. More than 11000 persons received training in a span of one year. The trainers drafted the resource materials with the help of various experts and professionals and utilized the material for training and capacity building.

The list of resource materials produced in this project include the following:

- Investigation of trafficking crimes for sexual exploitation.
- SOP on the investigation of trafficking crimes for exploitative labour.
- Protocol for interstate transfer of trafficked victims.
- Manual for psycho-social intervention.
- Manual for training police on anti-human trafficking.
- Manual for training prosecutors on anti-human trafficking.
- Compendium of best practices by NGOs on anti-human trafficking.
- Compendium of best practices by Indian Police on the issue.
- Handbook for Indian police to address human trafficking crimes.

- Protocol on setting up Integrated anti-human trafficking units in India.
- Compendium on the legal framework.
- Posters on eight themes on trafficking.
- Film on anti-human trafficking, titled One Life, No Price, a documentary of seven minutes, with Amitabh Bachchan, Priety Zinta and John Abraham as actors.

Impact of AHTU

The initiative of building synergy among the stakeholders and providing appropriate response to human trafficking brought in several expected and even unexpected results. Trained police officers and other stakeholders ensured holistic response related to action, including prevention, protection and prosecution. The number of arrests, prosecutions and convictions of traffickers and exploiters shot up. This had several implications, for example:

- The fact that enforcement became effective
- Conviction of offenders perceived as an effective need and tool for prevention of trafficking.
- Every convicted person has no opportunity to traffic any more victim. Therefore, one conviction means several crimes prevented.
- A message to the traffickers that they cannot escape the law. The punishment awarded to the convicted persons went up.
- The number of persons rescued increased phenomenally and among them, the percentage of children went up. This showed the commitment and dedication brought about in addressing the issue.

- Victimisation of victims became part of history. The AHTU ensured that they take proper care of the rescued persons.
- Law enforcement with the arrest of a large number of customers. Customers' are those who sexually exploit the trafficked women.

ITP ACT CASES IN AP STATE RECORDED DURING THE FIRST HALF OF THE YEAR 2007 (Jan to June 2007) WITH CORRESPONDING PERIOD OF PREVIOUS YEAR

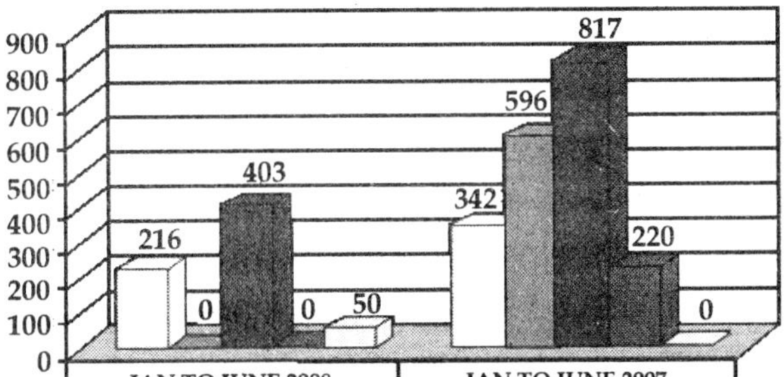

	JAN TO JUNE 2008	JAN TO JUNE 2007
No. of cases registered	216	342
Victims rescued	0	596
Traffoclers arrested	403	817
Customers arrested	0	220
Arrests u/s 8 ITP Act	50	0

After appraising the situation, empowerment process created a paradigm shift. AHTU helped to nab all offenders, including those who create, perpetuate and sustain 'demand'.

Closing down places of exploitation: The Immoral Traffic Prevention Act 1956 had remained largely unutilized and several law enforcement officials were unaware of this Act. The law is very potent as the sub-divisional magistrate can order closure and eviction of the premises used for exploitation even before the conviction of the offender by a judicial court. Moreover, the order of closure/ eviction neither can be appealed against, nor stayed nor challenged. (Refer Section 18(3) of ITPA).

A comparison of the scenario before and after training is worth highlighting. The data from AP police quoted below is self-explanatory as it shows a clear paradigm shift after the training.

Witness Protection Measures: AHTU felt the need to protect the witnesses afraid of deposing in the court. Accordingly, the trained police officials and NGOs have started using several witness protection measures including counselling of witnesses before they are produced in the court. A classic example is that in Andhra Pradesh where the lone witness (victim) was reluctant to attend the court, but after continuous counselling by the NGO member and the woman police official, both members of the AHTU the witness deposed in the court and this led to the conviction of the trafficker.

Victim Protection Measures: One of the remarkable achievements of the teamwork developed by AHTU is that the law enforcement machinery started seeing victims of trafficking as victims of organized crime. Moreover, the networking with the government agencies and the NGOs has given rise to innumerable rehabilitation programmes. Linkages with corporate have also been activated, who are providing sustainable livelihood to the rescued persons.

Non-victimization of victims: The AHTU and the capacity building process proved a revelation for the police officials who were earlier sending both the trafficked and the trafficker to jail. As a direct result of the empowerment process, they were able to differentiate between the two and take steps to protect the victims. In fact, victimization of victims was a bane in law enforcement in India, as was the case elsewhere. One of the major impacts in the AHTU-sponsored synergy is to put a stop to this menace of victimizing the victims. They should be treated as they are, i.e. as victims of human trafficking.

Change in Priority: Any response system has a method of prioritizing issues and responding according to the priority. In the existing law enforcement scenario and the justice delivery process, anti-human trafficking was nowhere in the reckoning. It was never a priority. One's perceptions dictate this, both perception of oneself about others and perception of one about other's perception of self. The human rights approach and the paradigm of "seeing things from the best interest of the victim" have made a transformation in the minds of the law enforcement officials. Those who were always seeing the world from one's views started seeing oneself from the views of the world. This is indeed an achievement in ensuring a positive attitudinal orientation.

Attitudinal Change: One of the most important changes brought about by the AHTU and related activities in the project are the attitudinal change of the stakeholders, especially the responders. Some of the changes are as follows:

- Change in recognition of human trafficking (HT) as an act of violation of human rights and dignity.
- Change in recognizing HT as an organised crime.

- Change in the style of investigation, especially in investigating it from the organized crime perspective.
- Change in the priority attributed to the offence of human trafficking.
- Change in the treatment meted out to victims.
- Change in recognizing them as victims and not offenders.
- Change in accepting role of NGOs in law enforcement.
- Change in accepting NGOs as partners in response.
- Change in recognizing the good work done by police, prosecutors, medical professionals, counsellors, etc.

An interesting aspect of the attitudinal change is that the changes descend from the top. The people at the top levels of response agencies made conscientious efforts to cooperate with AHTU to address the issues of human trafficking. Indeed the AHTU did take a large number of steps to bring about a positive and rights-oriented approach towards the victims of human trafficking.

Help Seeking Behaviour: Because of the teamwork of AHTU, coupled with the training and capacity building workshops, there is a positive change by way of the growing positive indulgence among the police, prosecutors, government agencies, NGOs, civil society and the media. Police officials have opened up their doors to NGOs They are utilizing the network developed through the training process for taking help of NGOs in all activities starting with rescue and post-rescue care as well as on prevention. NGOs have now become integral part of the training and capacity building process.

Help Rendering Behaviour: Anti-human trafficking is an area where NGOs can and do have a lot to do, despite the fact that it is the responsibility of the government agencies, law enforcement and rehabilitation departments. The activities of AHTU have sent out a message to the NGOs that they are partners in action. Moreover, NGOs are putting to use this alliance in extending all support to the law enforcement agencies in prevention, protection and prosecution. Many NGOs are coming forth with intelligence and information of traffickers.

Developing and Harnessing Human Potential: During the trainings, they focused on a comprehensive package of KSAR (knowledge, skills, attitudinal orientation and resources). The effort was to develop human capital from the mass of law enforcement officials. Stimulating discussions and activities involving thinkers, doers, deliverers, performers, and achievers propelled the human development thus providing a solid and deliberate recipe for human capital

Prevention of Human Trafficking: The law enforcement agencies, as a part of the AHTU, started giving more stress on prevention of human trafficking. Police officials have developed networks with the representatives of grass-roots democracy (Panchayat Raj Institutions), paralegal volunteers etc. and have undertaken several activities to address the vulnerability factors. This has increased public awareness against human trafficking.

Community Policing on Human Trafficking: The community policing means the involvement of the civilians and police to work as a team to forestall the incidences of human trafficking. A community and a police working together is a community-oriented and community- driven teamwork.

Visibility: The visibility is obvious from the media reports and the interest generated among the various stakeholders including political personalities on issues of human trafficking. This has given rise to timely appreciation of the meaningful initiatives undertaken by the law enforcement agencies. The public appreciation has, in fact, enhanced their morale and output and prompted them for better delivery.

Public support in sharing intelligence on traffickers and offenders: The teamwork in AHTU along with the public appreciation of the activities especially through the media has brought in tremendous public support to the law enforcement agencies, especially in matters of information and intelligence. The police have registered several crimes based on the source information provided by the public and many crimes prevented based on the timely inputs from the public.

Demand for extension of the project to other States: The public have taken note of the achievements of AHTU in the project and have appreciated. As a result, there is consistent demand for setting up more AHTUs in the project states and for extension of the same to other states, so far not covered under the project.

Involvement of the media in Anti-Human Trafficking: The role of media has been observed on three fronts, viz. in ensuring that the media reporting does not violate the rights of victims, in generating public appreciation for the good work done by the response agencies and in creating public awareness leading to prevention of human trafficking. The media personnel came to realize the importance of maintaining the anonymity of the victims.

Involvement of the corporate in Anti-Human Trafficking: The AHTUs have taken several steps well beyond the normative mandate. Corporate and business houses have taken keen interest in anti-human trafficking activities. Several corporate have joined the process, not only in the rehabilitation of the trafficked victims but also in undertaking public awareness programmes and prevention activities at the source areas.

Multi-Stakeholder Linkages and Involvement: Presently, numerous agencies from different occupations are taking keen interest in the anti-human trafficking mission. This includes different government departments, like home, women and child, health, labour, social justice, prosecution, police, civil defence as well as other UN agencies, NGOs and other civil society partners, social activists, lawyers, judges, jurists, academics, corporate, business houses, media, political personalities, professional bodies like Indian Medical Association, religious congregations like the Catholic Relief Services, Church of North India, etc.

Involvement of the political leaders in Anti-Human Trafficking: The chief ministers of the states where anti-human trafficking units were established have assured commitment to anti-human trafficking and all support in the process. The involvement and concern of the political leaders in the states, especially Goa, Andhra Pradesh, Bihar and West Bengal have been instrumental in providing the appropriate impetus and initiative to the law enforcement machinery to take effective steps in preventing and combating human trafficking. The political initiative has, in fact, been the real catalyst for action.

Assessment: The external evaluators Dr Sarala Gopalan and Professor Laura Livingston evaluated the various activities of the Project, including the functioning of the AHTUs. In their report (available with UNODC, New Delhi), they arrived at a conclusion that AHTU is a paradigm example of innovative thinking and action in addressing human trafficking. The functioning of AHTU in the states demonstrated that the AHTU is the best model in the given situation to address human trafficking in a comprehensive and sustained manner. The letter from MHA dated 16 November 2007 addressed to the home secretaries of all states reads, "The Project (UNODC) has had very positive outcomes in some of the states and the Anti-Human Trafficking Unit model has been particularly effective. The Project has also generated some very useful products in the form of training manuals and Standard Operating Procedures for investigation and rescue in trafficking cases. It is, therefore worthwhile to extend the AHTU model to all the Districts of the country and utilize the training manuals and SOPs under the proposed Centrally Sponsored Scheme for TOT and AHTU". The government proposed that by the end of the present five-year plan, at least 297 AHTUs would be set up. This is indeed a certificate of recognition of the performance of AHTU. They

UNODC operated the project in collaboration with the Government of India, the state government agencies and civil society groups.

AHTU in Problem-Oriented Policing: AHTU is a paradigm of combined efforts. It brings all stakeholders together in the common cause. They undertake integrated action. The activities include of prevention, protection and prosecution. Therefore, it addresses the problem in its entirety.

To sum up, anti-human trafficking unit (AHTU) is an embodiment, an institution and a living example of so many qualities and functionalities, including the following:

- Out-of-the-box thinking in addressing a grave issue.
- Transformation of individuals through capacity building and empowerment.
- Institutionalization of a best practice.
- Putting on top agenda an issue, which was never in the agenda?
- Building up a team of stakeholders through consultative process and orienting the alliance for the best delivery.
- Addressing a grave human rights problem from the perspective of problem-oriented policing.

11

Welfare of Policemen

Need for Revamp

Ajay Kashyap, IPS*

ORGANIZATION OF ADEQUATE welfare measures for police personnel and their families is a must for the maintenance of their morale in the midst of difficult and taxing working conditions.

The Delhi Police commission has mentioned in its report that, "In order to maintain a high standard of discipline in an organized force, it is essential to pay a great deal of attention to the welfare of the men and the members of their families and to provide them with various amenities to make their otherwise hard and monotonous lives bearable."

All over the world, a great deal of emphasis is laid on the welfare of the men in the police and this is one

* The writer was Joint Commissioner, Delhi Police and presently posted with United Nations

The author shaking hands with YS Dadwal, IPS, in presence of Karnal Singh, IPS, Amulya Patnaik, IPS, Mansur Ali Sayed, IPS and other police officers.

of the important factors which has contributed to the maintenance of good discipline in police forces. The necessity of welfare measures and amenities for the police, particularly in the lower ranks, has been stressed on many occasions by even such personalities as the Prime Minister and the Home Minister of India. Speaking at one of the conferences of Inspectors-General of Police, the late Prime Minister Pandit Jawaharlal Nehru said, "The question of conditions of service in the police force especially those for constables and others is important. Apart from the question of salaries and wages, it is important to remember that frequently a careful psychological approach gets much better results that even the little money."

According to a survey conducted by BPR&D in 1986 welfare facilities provided to police personnel fall under the following broad heads—

- Police Housing.
- Pensionary Benefits.
- Medical Facilities.
- Educational Facilities.
- Group Insurance and Savings Schemes.
- Resettlement of Retired Police Personnel.
- Special Entitlement for Leave.
- Police Welfare Funds.
- Police Welfare Officers.
- Family Welfare-cum-work centres.
- Canteens and Cooperative Stores.

On the face of it welfare schemes have generally concentrated at cash dole-outs aimed at partially or substantially meeting expenditures on various head and necessities including shelter, health, education and compensation to the next of kin in case of death. Schemes mostly concentrate on reimbursement of expenses (e.g. scholarship, educational grants, etc.) augmenting income through modest welfare projects, etc. Some of the larger forces have set up education institutions like schools, ITIs, etc, with reservation of admission for police wards to meet the requirement of quality education and training to these wards. Insurance and risk cover are relatively new areas where police welfare has made initial strides. There has been however a singular lack of imagination in assessing the holistic needs of policeman during his span of service averaging 30 years or more and his requirements after post retirement.

Life Cycle

An average career can be divided into three distinct phases. Each phase has distinctive peculiarities while together govern his vulnerability. Factors like personal and family profile, organizational status, earnings, savings, etc. In the first phase (10-15 years of service), the employee enjoys excellent state of health for himself and family. His family commitments in terms of needs of dependents (education/marriage of children, settlement of dependents, bereavement, etc.) are non-existent or minimal. This period is marked by induction/initial training, minimal organizational stress. While earnings are at the lower end of pay scale, the propensity to save is quite high.

In the second phase of life cycle (15-25 years) the vulnerability factors in terms of health remain sound, the presence of family commitments is moderate/increases, while the propensity to save remains high. Organisational stress remains moderate.

VULNERABILITY FACTORS IN DIFFERENT PHASE OF EACH INDIVIDUAL

	First Phase	Second Phase	Third Phase
No. of years service life	10-15	15-25	25-35
Health (of self and spouse)	Excellent	V. good	Declining
Family commitments (Own/Children marriage/settlement/bereavement etc)	Minimal	Moderate	High
Organizational stress	Minimal	Moderate	High
Earnings	Minimal	Marginally higher	Higher
Propensity to Save	Highest	Declines marginally but still high	Moderate or low due to liabilities
Counselling Needs	Family Planning Savings Plan Stress management	Stress Management	Post-retrial skills Stress management Psychological counselling

In the third phase (25-35 years), declining health, pressing family commitments, greater organizational stress place severe pressures on the vulnerability of individual.

An understanding of welfare needs of a policeman in each phase of this life cycle would be different and ideally the welfare policy of the organization should recognize and proactively address these needs. Preparing the police officer for a fruitful and fulfilling post retrial life is an aspect of police welfare that has remained largely neglected.

In 1967, two social scientists devised a Social Readjustment Rating Scale which rates the most common cause of stress in a persons life on a scale of 1-100. Prepared from environments in Westerns countries, this scale rated retirement (45%) as a serious stressor. Obviously, in more competitive scenario prevailing in the developed world, the impact of retirement from service will certainly be more powerful on individuals.

Retirement can prove a major stressor in life. A holistic approach would consider retirement not as an end itself but a start of a new beginning. Some opt to take it easy upon retirement and spend time with their families. Others transit into a second career, enriched with experiences acquired in their career with police.

To enjoy a smooth transition into a second career or retirement, each individual should take charge and plan well ahead.

The highest vulnerability faced by an employee is in the third life cycle. In this phase the welfare function should focus on equipping the employee to imbibe post retirement skills for reemployment/rehabilitation after superannuation along with aggressive stress management performances.

One of the most successful career transition framework have to be developed by Singapore Police Force where pre-retirement programmes are customized to the needs of officers with respect of their retirement from one force career transition programmes are conducted in five stages.

Stage 1 : Psychological and Mental Preparation for Retirement (4-5 years before)

Stage 2 : Generic Programmes (3-5 years before)

Stage 3 : Specialised Programmes (1-2 years before)

Stage 4 : Engagement of Officers on Post-Retirement Options (1 year before)

Stage 5 : Facilitating and Sharing of Jobs Opportunities Information. Encourage Officers to join Singapore Police Retirees' Association to expand network (1–6 months before retirement and beyond retirement)

Successful Transition to Retirement or Second Career

- Making psychological changes
- Staying healthy
- Harvesting your financial gains
- Searching for your second career
- Getting the job
- Starting your own business

Psychological preparation and counseling are essential for a successful transition to retirement or a second career. In addition the policeman has to be prepared for maintaining health, conservative financial planning to enjoy life long financial security, entrepreneurial skills where needed. He has to be taught to leverage the managerial skills imbibed during his service including public relation, human resources, corporate planning, investigations, event management, etc. These experiences and skills gained in course of his service with the force stand his in good stead in post retrial phase of his life.

The author and his wife meeting the President Smt. Pratibha Patil alongwith YS Dadwal, IPS, and Rajan Bhagat, PRO-Delhi Police.

The police needs to proactively project the strengths of the retiring employees to prospective employers. The welfare function should also facilitate job function by maintaining close and real time interface with stake holders life industry association etc.

Bibliography

1. Holmes TH, Rahe RH (1967). "The Social Readjustment Rating Scale". J. Psychosom Res 11(2):213-8 doi:10.1016/0022-3999(67)90010-4. PMID 6059863.
2. Rahe RH, Mahan JL, Arthur RJ (1970). "Prediction of near-future health change from subjects' preceding life changes". J. Psychosom Res 14(4):401-6 doi:10.1016/0022-3999(70) 90008-5. PMID 549561.
3. A.H.Maslow, A Theory of Human Motivation, *Psychological Review* 50(4) (1943):L370-96.
4. Maslow, Abraham (1954). Motivation and Personality. New York: Harper. pp236.
5. Report of Delhi Police Commission, 1966-68 Volume-1.
6. First Report of the National Police Commission, GOI, February, 1979.
7. A Survey conducted by BPR&D in 1986.
8. Study on Welfare Schemes in CRPF.

12

India's Internal Security

Dr Manmohan Singh
Prime Minister of India

AS FAR AS TERRORISM is concerned, during the past year we have achieved some major successes. Many terrorist modules have been dismantled and arrests of several important terrorists have taken place. It is on account of your alertness that we have not had a serious terrorist attack since November 2008. But our success in preventing terrorist attacks can be sustained only at the price of unrelenting vigilance. There are many developments taking place in our country and outside which have a bearing on our internal security. It is important to understand their true nature and the exact way they can and they could affect us. We also need to understand better why many more local youth are being induced into participating in terrorist activities and how they are being recruited, indoctrinated and trained.

The Prime Minister, Dr. Manmohan Singh addressing the DGPs/IGPs Conference in New Delhi on 15 September 2009.

(Photo: PIB)

The factors that cause social disharmony and alienation should be clearly known so that we can work to eliminate them. I urge you to pay particular attention to these aspects.

I have consistently held that in many ways, the Left Wing extremism is, perhaps, the gravest internal security threat our country faces. We have discussed this in the last five years and I would like to say frankly that we have not achieved as much success as we would have liked in containing this menace. It is a matter of concern that despite our efforts, the level of violence in the affected States continues to rise.

As I have stated before, dealing with Left Wing extremism requires a nuanced strategy, a holistic approach, it cannot be treated simply as a law and order problem. Despite its sanguinary nature, the movement manages to retain the support of a section of the tribal communities and the poorest of the poor in many affected areas. It has influence among certain sections of the civil society, the intelligentsia and the youth. It still retains a certain élan. All this adds to the complexity of the problem. I expect you to keep this in mind as you devise newer and better strategies to deal with this problem.

The situation in the North-Eastern parts of our country is also far from comfortable. In two of the States, viz., Manipur and Assam, current levels of violence give us cause for concern. In addition, extortion and intimidation have become a menace across most of the States in the region and they have reached a point where they constitute a serious hampering of the implementation of a number of development projects in these States. I believe it should be possible to bring about a substantial improvement in the situation if there is better security management. I would, therefore, enjoin upon the DGsP of the States in the North-East to insist upon, and achieve, higher levels of professionalism from the Forces they command. Firm but compassionate handling of law and order matters, can certainly bring about substantial improvement in the prevailing state of affairs. Particularly so, as in terms of number, we are dealing with a very limited number of people who have gone stray. If we do not and we cannot deal with them at the present stage of our development, it might be more difficult at a later date to tame these evil forces.

In the case of Jammu & Kashmir, we have reasons to be satisfied that elections to both the State Assembly and our Parliament during the past year were held in a peaceful atmosphere. The level of violence in the State has also come down and is perhaps at its lowest level since the beginning of insurgency in the late '80s.

But there is no scope for complacency. There are certain developments that are worrisome. Infiltration across the Line of Control and also via other routes such as Nepal, Bangladesh and the sea is going up. Encounters with armed militants have become more frequent in recent weeks and months. Secessionist and militant groups within the State are once again attempting to make common cause with outside elements and have embarked on a series of protest movements. The intention apparently is to create an impression of widespread turmoil in the State. We must not and I repeat we must not allow such a situation to develop. It is imperative that these disruptive efforts are contained, controlled and effectively checked.

I would like to compliment my friend, the Home Minister and his team for the efforts they have made in the last many months to improve our internal security situation. I am happy that action is being taken on the report of the task force that I had announced in this very last conference. This, together with the Action Plans drawn up by the Home Ministry, should go a long way to improve police performance, make the security Agencies more responsive to terrorist threats and improve their overall efficiency.

I would particularly like to recommend to you the idea of our agencies developing strategic foresight to anticipate future surprise attacks like the one that took place in Mumbai in November last year. Improved intelligence generation and coordination are critical to developing such a capability. Also, like in other areas of governance, new technology and technological innovations can go a very long way in improving our performance in all dimensions of the internal security challenges. I am confident that the establishment of a secure net-centric information command structure would substantially improve the capabilities of our Agencies to deal with the internal security challenges.

Let me now move to certain areas in which the Central and State Governments need to take quick action. It is absolutely imperative that we strengthen policing at the grassroots level. The Police Station has to be the fulcrum around which this needs to take place. A large increase in the number of Police Stations along with raising the strength of Police Stations has to be undertaken. We need far higher numbers of policemen and policewomen to improve the present low police-population ratio of 145 per hundred thousand of population. As a first step, I would urge all of you to do everything possible to fill up the large number of vacancies that exist today at various levels in our police force. At the same time greater attention has to be paid to the provision of adequate amenities for the constables and I would like to particularly emphasize a provision of housing facilities for our policemen. A situation that a large number of policemen are compelled to make private arrangements for renting houses is fraught with serious problems, particularly, from the view point of enforcement of effective law and order.

But increasing numbers will not be enough. We need a new-age policeman who is more professional, better-motivated, suitably empowered, well-trained, one who places greater emphasis on technology for investigation and other tasks. Emphasis should be on capacity building from the police station level itself, so that the police are better equipped. Each police station should aim at being self-sufficient and needs to be given the required resources in terms of anti-riot gear, better weapons, and the nucleus of a mobile forensic unit and be connected to a networked criminal data base management system. Every city should have a modern police control room with digitized maps. The key here lies in the plans for the modernization of our Police force. I am aware that the Police modernization framework is being substantially enlarged, but I would still urge that modernization of the Police should receive the highest priority. Our police forces must operate on the frontiers of modern technology. We must also design systems and procedures which will minimize scope for corruption. We should have a sufficiently long-term perspective in this area and also the required amount of funds should be made available for the purpose.

I must specially emphasize here the critical importance of training for policemen. I understand that on the average a Police officer is retrained only once in about twenty years. This is totally inadequate in the changed circumstances and this must be rectified. It would also help if the police were to benchmark their training curricula with the syllabi and training methodologies of Police training institutions elsewhere in the world to ensure better quality. The world is changing and changing very rapidly and Police training must keep pace with the best practices being followed in the world.

Today, there is little research in subjects related to the police and policing. An analytical approach to the problems and difficulties that come in the way of better policing could prove extremely useful. I would like the proposals for the setting up of a National Police University and also of a National Institute for Law and Order-related subjects to be pursued more vigorously. We need first-rate institutions to come up, which are capable of looking at all such issues in a truly holistic manner paying particular attention to problems of effective policing in rural areas as well as in major metropolitan cities and thereby create a body of literature on all these vital subjects.

Indeed, it is your solemn duty to protect the weak and the defenceless. Those who seek to promote communal violence and discord have to be dealt with firmly. Special efforts must be made to establish a relationship of trust and confidence between our police forces and the minority communities. You must not fail in this aspect. The underprivileged and weaker sections of our society- the minorities, the SCs and STs, women and senior citizens- should feel adequate confidence in the ability of our police force to protect. The common man should go about his daily life with a sense of security. He should have faith in the policeman and the police station. And this I believe is the real test of our efforts, a test that we cannot afford to fail."

(Source: Excerpts from the PM's address at the DGPs and IGPs Conference 2009)

13

Internal Security

P Chidambaram
Home Minister of India

IN THE LAST SEVEN MONTHS the Central Government has, with your co-operation and support, delivered on many promises. There has been no terrorist attack after the horrific crimes committed in Mumbai last November. We were able to hold the elections to Parliament; they were orderly and peaceful, barring a few pre-meditated attacks by Naxalites. The Amarnath Yatra, spread over 52 days ended without incident and 3,82,512 persons were able to complete the pilgrimage. Independence Day 2009 passed off peacefully in all the States. Yesterday, the World Badminton Championships came to an end without a hitch, proving that India has the capacity to provide full security for international sporting events.

The Union Home Minister, Shri P. Chidambaram addressing at the Chief Ministers' Conference on Internal Security, in New Delhi on 17 August 2009.

(Photo: PIB)

Let me recall the three challenges to internal security: firstly, terrorism; secondly, insurgency in the North Eastern States; and thirdly, Left wing extremism or Naxalism. Each one of them shares many characteristics with the other two; at the same time, each one of them is significantly different from the other two. We have one instrument to confront and defeat the three challenges, and that is the police. In the final analysis, it is the policeman and the policewoman who will help us win these battles. To that policeman and policewoman, this conference must send out a clear message that Government at every level is duty bound to provide them every kind of support, monetary, material and moral. Let us never forget that more than any other branch of government; it is the police that has paid the highest price in terms of human lives that have been lost. In the 7 ½ months of calendar 2009, 303 men and women belonging to the police and paramilitary forces have laid down their lives, and I know that you will join me in saluting their supreme sacrifice.

Let me briefly deal with the three challenges, and I begin with terrorism. It is a matter of satisfaction that eight months have passed since the last terrorist attack. However, I hasten to add that it does not mean that the threat of terror has vanished or receded. It is better intelligence and better preparedness that have helped us thwart potential terror attacks. We have cracked several terror modules and made several significant arrests, but the gravity of the threat is undiminished. We cannot afford to lower our guard, and we shall not.

The second challenge is insurgency or militancy. The security situation in Jammu and Kashmir has shown perceptible improvement. Militancy has declined, even while agitational politics is on the rise. The Central Government has offered every support to the new State Government to maintain law and order, focus on development and find political solutions through dialogue. In the North East, insurgency remains a grave threat. In the last few months we have refined our policy stance: the law will be applied strictly; ceasefire agreements will be enforced in letter and spirit; and we will talk to any group only if that group abjures violence, lays down its arms and offers to surrender. I regret to say that I cannot report much progress in the North Eastern States. At times, we find that some State Governments have allowed themselves to bend before insurgent groups, making the fight against insurgency that much more difficult. I propose to hold discussions with the State Governments concerned and draw up State-specific strategies to deal with the insurgent groups in the three most affected States of Assam, Nagaland and Manipur.

The third challenge is Left wing extremism or Naxalism. On more than one occasion, the Prime Minister had rightly cautioned the nation that Left wing extremism posed the "single biggest internal security challenge" to India. In the last few months, the CPI (Maoist) has stepped up its attacks on the Indian State and on the Indian people. I would like to draw your attention to a document put out by the CPI (Maoist) on June 12, 2009 which is titled "Post-Election Situation, Our Tasks". Anyone reading that document would have no illusion about the nature and gravity of the threat. Let me make our policy stance clear: We believe in the two-pronged approach of development and police action. However, the Naxalites are anti-development and have targeted the very instruments of development school buildings, roads, telephone towers, etc. They know that development will wean the masses, especially the poor tribals, away from the grip of the Naxalites. Hence, these deliberate attacks on developmental activities. Our response therefore will be police action to wrest control of territory that is now dominated by the Naxalites, restoration of civil administration and undertaking developmental activities in that order. Meanwhile, we will encourage State Governments to talk to the Naxalites both individuals and local units on condition that they give up their misconceived "armed liberation struggle". Let our message to the Naxalites be this: we will talk; we will act; we will restore order; and we will undertake developmental activities. I am happy to report that all the Naxal affected States have resolved to confront and overcome the challenge of the CPI (Maoist), and later this evening I shall hold a separate meeting with the Governor and Chief Ministers of those States.

When I look back on the last seven months, I find that our collective record has been a mixed one. Our best achievements have been in the reiteration of our determination to fight terror; in the sharing of intelligence; in the unanimous support for new laws and new instruments; and in acknowledging that police reforms have been neglected for too long. On the other hand, there are still critical deficiencies in budget allocations for the police, recruitment, training, procurement of equipment, introduction of technology, and personnel management.

I may now turn to the tasks ahead, especially the task of removing the deficiencies that I highlighted just now. While preparing for this conference, we had circulated a questionnaire to the State Governments requesting them to indicate the present status under a number of heads and on a number of issues. I regret to point out that the response from the States is far from satisfactory, and I am sure Chief Ministers would have reached more or less the same conclusion. I therefore wish to list the more important concerns so that the Heads of Delegation may, during their interventions, address the conference on these issues.

- The situation of vacant posts in the police is quite alarming. As on 01 January 2008, 230,567 posts were vacant against the total sanctioned strength of the States' police forces, both civil and armed. It is possible that the situation has improved since. The State Governments may wish to highlight the progress made in this regard.
- With the setting up of the Multi-Agency Centre (MAC) and S-MACs, intelligence sharing has improved, but there is scope for improvement in intelligence gathering. At the last conference, we had circulated a scheme for strengthening the State Special Branch (SSB). Some decisions have been taken at a meeting with representatives of State Governments on July 2, 2009. The State Governments may wish to address issues like creation of a separate cadre for intelligence; filling the vacancies in the SSB; revision of special branch manual; appointment of a dedicated intelligence officer in each police station; and reactivating the beat constable system.
- While NSG hubs have been set up in four cities and Special Forces units have been located in two cities, there is a need for State Governments to raise and deploy their own special intervention units (SIUs) and quick reaction teams (QRTs) in as many cities as possible. It is also necessary to put in place a clear command structure in the case of a terrorist threat or terrorist attack. The State Governments may wish to address the conference on the steps taken in this regard.
- We had commended to the States the idea of raising a State Industrial Security Force on the pattern of

the Central Industrial Security Force. There are multiple benefits in raising such a force, and I would request the State Governments to respond to the suggestion.

There is a new focus on coastal security and border management. However, we are concerned about the slow pace of construction of coastal police stations, outposts and checkposts as well as border outposts (BoPs) along the land border; constitution of State Maritime Boards, registration of vessels, issue of ID cards to fishermen, and utilisation of interceptor speed boats. The State Governments may wish to share their thoughts on how the pace of implementation can be quickened and the gaps in security plugged.

The Modernization of Police Forces (MPF) scheme is being implemented since 2000-2001. A C&AG report made in January 2009 has highlighted crucial deficiencies. I request State Governments to share with us urgently the Action Taken Report on the audit findings of the C&AG.

Police reforms have not received the attention they deserve. The Supreme Court has issued certain directions in the case of Prakash Singh and Others Vs Union of India and has appointed the Justice Thomas Committee to monitor compliance with those directions. I regret to point out that many State Governments have not yet constituted the Police Establishment Board. Nor have they fully complied with the other directions. The State Governments may wish to share with us the steps taken by them in the matter of police reforms.

The State Governments and the Central Government share an onerous responsibility. Nothing is more important to ensure the welfare of the people than the assurance of security. And none can contribute more to this sense of security than the State Governments. You have the constitutional power and responsibility in respect of matters relating to 'public order' and 'police'. However, increasingly, jurists and the general public have emphasized the constitutional duty of the Central Government to 'protect every State against internal disturbance'. Hence, the need for the Central Government and the State Governments to work together in a spirit of partnership."

(Source: Excerpts from the address by the Home Minister at the conference of Chief Ministers on Internal Security, 17 August 2009)

Index

Notes

Notes

Notes

Notes